WORLDWIDE WORSHIP

WORLDWIDE WORSHIP

PRAYERS, SONGS, AND POETRY

Edited by
John Marks Templeton

TEMPLETON FOUNDATION PRESS
PHILADELPHIA & LONDON

Templeton Foundation Press
Five Radnor Corporate Center, Suite 120
100 Matsonford Road
Radnor, Pennsylvania 19087

Library of Congress Cataloging-in-Publication Data

Templeton, John, 1912–
    Worldwide worship : prayers, songs, and poetry /
    John Marks Templeton
    p. cm.
    Includes bibliographical references and index.
    ISBN 1-890151-35-1 (hard cover : alk. paper)
        1. Prayers. I. Title

    BL560 .T46 2000
    291.4'33—dc21   00-020280

Cover design by Gopa & the Bear
Interior designed and typeset by Gopa Design
Printed in the United States of America

00 01 02 03 04 05 06   10 9 8 7 6 5 4 3 2 1

Contents

PART 2. UNIVERSAL SPIRITUAL SONGS

Part 3. Truth the Poet Speaks

PART 4. LET EVERY HEART WORSHIP OUR CREATOR

Acknowledgment of Sources

WORLDWIDE WORSHIP

Prayers, Songs, and Poetry

INTRODUCTION

ONE OF THE MAIN GUIDELINES of the programs of the John Templeton Foundation can be described as the "theology of humility." The theology of humility is not man-centered but God-centered. It proposes that the infinite God may not even be adequately describable in human words and concepts and may not be restricted by human rationality. Perhaps God is not limited by our senses or by our perceptions of three dimensions in space or one dimension in time. Perhaps there was no absolute beginning and there will be no absolute end, but only everlasting change and variety in the unlimited purposes, freedom, and creativity of God.

Humility can be a key to progress. We know so little and need to learn so much. Inasmuch as every person's concept of God is too small, through humility and a sincere desire to learn we can begin to realize the infinity of God. We can also become more understanding and loving of ourselves and of our fellow human beings on life's educational journey.

My purpose in assembling this collection of poems, prayers, prose, and hymns from various world cultures and religions is to share some of the works of inspiration that I find especially beautiful or affecting that can assist us in learning various lessons of life. Human nature seems to be such that both children and adults can better remember when worshipful concepts are expressed in these avenues. Many of these selections express the vastly larger concepts of God suggested by humility in theology.

One may wonder, what profit is found in studying the wisdom passed along to us? Why not simply live from day to day, taking things as they come? One answer is that our stay on planet Earth is a brief one and the time we are given to educate ourselves is all too short. For each person to grow spiritually, it is important to learn from others who may be wiser than we are. From excellent writers we can come to realize the impact of even a small gesture, word, or action upon our self or another person, upon our community, and, yes, even upon our world.

There can also be comfort in reading inspired thoughts from the great thinkers and writers from various cultures and religious perspectives. These timeless formulas can form a bridge of enlightenment and enhanced awareness between today's reader and those faithful souls who literally "put their hearts on paper"!

Many passages selected for this book have numerous applications for thoughts for daily living. The words that can provide us with hope, inspiration, courage, consolation, consideration, joy, happiness, and perhaps a greater awareness of love come from all faiths and represent writers from various periods of history. In a variety of ways these writers present a message that God is love, always ready to radiate that love and wisdom throughout all of Creation. At this present moment, the human race, even after thousands of years, is still at the dawn of new creation. This is both tremendously exciting and an awe-inspiring responsibility! It is my hope that you, the reader, may draw inspiration and enthusiasm from these words and that perhaps some special passage may point the way toward a brighter, more useful, and meaningful future for you and others worldwide.

One thing we can learn from these wise writings is the power of prayers. One meaning of the term prayer is "to trap a thought." As one holds a thought it can become a state of mind or a generally held attitude. A personal, cultural, or spiritual approach to prayer relates to a concept of God and God's creative process. Regardless of what you do in life—enrolling in college, starting a business, buying stock, preparing a tax return, buying a home, having a tooth extracted, getting a job—you can do it better if you start with prayer. And let your prayer be that God will use you as a conduit for His love and wisdom. Let the words you speak and the actions you take be in harmony with God's purpose. Prayer can assist in creating an attitude from which true faith and conviction can grow. Many traditions have taught men and women to go beyond words into "the Silence"—a place of spiritual communion much deeper and more delicate to the soul than mere words.

Poetry has always held a proud place in the great pantheon of literature. Through the writings of the poet, the voices from all aspects of life ring loud and clear. In some instances, the sonorous meter, the proliferation of descriptive imagery, and the gentle didactic tones seemingly bespeak an uncomplicated muse. Poems are important because they push beyond the simplifications we use every day. One person can say to another, "I love you." And what is really meant by the words? One simple phrase is being used to label a thousand different sensations! One poem that I enjoy and included in this volume is "A Psalm of Life" by Henry Wadsworth Longfellow. It is subtitled, "What the heart of the young man said to the Psalmist." Food for thought! Down through the ages the poet spoke ... and the people listened. They are listening still!

Hymns from the world religions are filled with inspirational literature. One of my favorites is "Take Time to Be Holy." The soothing melody and gentle words of this beautiful hymn can be a precious reminder of the importance of "putting first things first" in our lives. Some hymns are so powerful and touch us in such a way that even the most mundane detail of our lives can become an encounter with the ultimate. They can be tremendous teaching aids as well as a source of pleasure and solace. Although the words of the hymns presented in this book are memorable, combining them in context with their music lends an even greater meaning to their message.

When the written word is expressed without bias, it can often paint a magnificent panorama of aspirations, inspirations, and, perhaps, universal guidance. Ideas of giving and receiving, understanding the power of the mind, experiencing the richness of living the spiritual life through prayer and praise, developing a humble attitude—all these things, and more, can be powerful building blocks in the foundation of a fulfilled and productive existence on earth. And being open to learning about the cultural and religious traditions of people whose beliefs may differ from ours can help us see that there are many valid paths to the Divine. So let us lead a compassionate life by transcending the demands of the clamorous ego and recognizing the sacredness in others and in all of life.

At the end of the book is a first-line index, a key-word index, an author index, and an acknowledgment of sources.

Poems, prayers, prose, and hymns! Take your time with this book—assimilate its words, ideas, and messages into your heart, soul, mind, and body; into your rest, relaxation, and meditation; into your worship ceremonies; into your relationships; into your ambitions, work, and play. Let the meaning of the words presented here flow over your soul, opening perhaps new avenues of awareness as you attune your mind to the rhythm of the cosmos. In doing this, you can be moved into a healthier, happier, richer, and more adventurous and purposeful way of living. And may you know that . . . God loves you, and I do, too!

John Marks Templeton

PART 1

A GATHERING OF PRAYERS

Prayer is a wondrous avenue for touching God and for experiencing what some may call "the attributes of God." The words of a deeply meaningful prayer may seem to literally vibrate with an energy that can stir the depths of the soul.

Over the years, it has become increasingly clear to me that every thought, feeling, and action is actually some kind of prayer. As we become more aware of this uplifting in consciousness, a kind of "divine intervention" may occur that provides us with more space to be silent and still. This can be a place where we bridge the gaps between fears and doubts—with love and serenity—where silent communion with God exists.

Prayer provides many blessings. It can offer a simple opportunity for a person to take another step forward. It can be a seemingly fleeting and tender awareness in one aspect of our life. Or it can be the thundering language of the soul, awakening our consciousness to some great spiritual truth. Prayer can provide an element of acceptance and surrender to the experiences in the journey of life in a powerful, transformational way. Prayer can also inspire us with enthusiasm to become helpers in God's accelerating creativity.

In whatever manner a person prays, prayer is a direct link with the Universal, the Total, the Absolute, God. Prayer can connect us with life as God, regardless of religious persuasion. From Africa, Australia, America, the Far East, India, and all the countries of the world, prayer provides an avenue in which men and women can experience the simple, sublime, and profoundly beautiful sense of connection to God and His purposes and to one another.

In the Beginning Was God

In the beginning was God,
Today is God,
Tomorrow will be God.
Who can make an image of God?
He has no body.
He is a word which comes out of your mouth.
That word! It is no more,
It is past, and it still lives!
So is God.

The Pygmies of the Congo recite this prayer,
which describes God as an eternal Spirit.

Prayer for Mankind

O Thou kind Lord! O Thou Who art generous and merciful! We are the servants of Thy threshold and are gathered beneath the sheltering shadow of Thy divine unity. The sun of Thy mercy is shining upon all, and the clouds of Thy bounty shower upon all. Thy gifts encompass all, Thy loving providence sustains all, Thy protection overshadows all. O Lord! Grant Thine infinite bestowals, and let the light of Thy guidance shine. Illumine the eyes, gladden the hearts with abiding joy. Confer a new spirit upon all people and bestow upon them eternal life. Unlock the gates of true understanding and let the light of faith shine resplendent. Gather all people beneath the shadow of Thy bounty and cause them to unite in harmony, so that they may become as the rays of one sun, as the waves of one ocean, and as the fruit of one tree. May they drink from the same fountain. May they be refreshed by the same breeze. May they receive illumination from the same source of light. Thou art the Giver, the Merciful, the Omnipotent.

'Abdu'l-Bahá

A Prayer

i thank You god for most this amazing
day:for the leading greenly spirits of trees
and a blue true dream of sky;and for everything
which is natural which is infinite which is yes.

(i who have died am alive again today,
and this is the sun's birthday;this is the birthday of life and of love and wings:and of the gay
great happening illimitably earth)

how should tasting touching hearing seeing
breathing any—lifted from the no
of all nothing—human merely being
doubt unimaginable You?

(now the ears of my ears awake and
now the eyes of my eyes are opened)

E. E. Cummings

A Vision of God

In the market, in the cloister—only God I saw.
In the valley and on the mountain—only God I saw.
Him I have seen beside me oft in tribulation;
In favor and in fortune—only God I saw.
In prayer and fasting, in praise and contemplation,
In the religion of the Prophet—only God I saw.
Neither soul nor body, accident nor substance,
Qualities nor causes—only God I saw.
Like a candle I was melting in His fire.
Amidst the flames outflashing—only God I saw.
I passed away into nothingness, I vanished,
And lo, I was the All-living—only God I saw.

Baba Kuhi of Shiraz

Sanskrit Salutation to the Dawn

Listen to the salutation to the dawn,
Look to this day for it is life, the very life of life,
In its brief course lie all the verities and realities
    of our existence.
The bliss of growth, the splendor of beauty,
For yesterday is but a dream and tomorrow is only a vision,
But today well spent makes every yesterday a dream
    of happiness
and every tomorrow a vision of hope.
Look well therefore to this day.
Such is the salutation to the dawn.

I must realize
That my God-satisfaction
Is only a prayer away.
Therefore, let me embark
On my prayer journey
Lovingly and confidently.

> *Sri Chinmoy*

Finding Prayer within Us

Whether He replies or not,
   Keep calling Him—
Ever calling in the chamber
   Of continuous prayer.
Whether He comes or not,
   Believe He is ever approaching
      Nearer to you
With each command of your heart's love.
   Whether He answers or not,
      Keep entreating Him.
   Even if He makes no reply
      In the way you expect,
Ever know that in some subtle way
      He will respond.
In the darkness of your deepest prayers,
   Know that with you He is playing
      Hide and seek.
And in the midst of His dance of life, disease, and death,
      If you keep calling Him,
   Undepressed by His seeming silence,
      You will receive His answer.

   Paramahansa Yogananda

Step softly, under snow or rain,
To find the place where men can pray;
The way is all so very plain
That we may lose the way.

      G. K. Chesterton

Islamic Verse of Light

God is the light of the heavens and the earth; the likeness of His
Light is as a niche wherein is a lamp. The lamp is in a glass, the
glass as it were a shining star, kindled from a blessed tree, an olive,
neither of the East nor of the West. Its oil would well-nigh shine,
even if no fire touched it. Light upon Light; God guides to His
Light whom He will. And God strikes similitudes for men, and
God has knowledge of all things.

Prayer at Midnight

O Lord and Master of my life,
give me not a spirit of sloth,
vain curiosity, lust for power and idle talk.

But give to me, your servant,
a spirit of soberness,
humility, patience, and love.

Yea, O Lord and King,
grant me to see my own faults,
and not to condemn my brother;
for blessed are you to the ages of ages. Amen.

    Saint Ephraim the Syrian

A Prayer in Spring

Oh, give us pleasure in the flowers today;
And give us not to think so far away
As the uncertain harvest; keep us here
All simply in the springing of the year.

Oh, give us pleasure in the orchard white,
Like nothing else by day, like ghosts by night;
And make us happy in the happy bees,
The swarm dilating round the perfect trees.

And make us happy in the darting bird
That suddenly above the bees is heard,
The meteor that thrusts in with needle bill,
And off a blossom in mid air stands still.

For this is love and nothing else is love,
The which it is reserved for God above
To sanctify to what far ends He will,
But which it only needs that we refill.

Robert Frost

Canticle of the Sun

Oh most high, potent, sweet Lord,
To you belong the praise, the glory, the honor
   and all blessing.

To you alone, Most High, they look for life,
And no man may fitly speak your Name.

With all your creatures, Lord, be praised,
Not least for our Brother Sun, who daily brings
   us light.

Beautiful and radiant in his great splendor
How well he tells of thee, Most High.

Be praised, my Lord, for Sister Moon and stars,
Carved by you, clear and rich and fair.

Be praised, my Lord, for Brother Wind,
For air in every mood and time through whom
   you give your creatures sustenance.

Be praised, my Lord, for Sister Water,
So useful, humble, precious and chaste.

Be praised, my Lord, for Brother Fire,
Which lightens us by night, fine and merry
   and healthy and strong.

Be praised, my Lord, for our Sister, Mother Earth,
Who holds us up and keeps us straight, yielding
   diverse fruits and flowers of different hue, and grass.

Be praised, my Lord, for those who find forgiveness
    in their hearts for your love's sake,
And bear sorrow and affliction.

Blessed are they who bear these in peace
Because by you, Most High, they will be crowned.

Praise be my Lord for our Sister mortal death,
From whom no man alive will escape.

Woe to those who die in mortal sin!

Blessed are those who are found walking
    in your most holy ways
For the second death will bring them no evil.

O praise and bless my Lord,
Thanking him and serving him with great humility.

Saint Francis of Assisi

Native American Prayer to the Four Directions

Spirit of the East, spirit of air,
of morning and springtime:
Be with us as the sun rises,
in times of beginning,
times of planting.
Inspire us with the fresh breath of courage
as we go forth into new adventures.

Spirit of the South, spirit of fire,
of noontime and summer:
Be with us through the heat of the day
and help us to be ever growing.
Warm us with strength
and energy for the work that awaits us.

Spirit of the West, spirit of water,
of evening and autumn:
Be with us as the sun sets
and help us to enjoy a rich harvest.
Flow through us with a cooling,
healing quietness and bring us peace.

Spirit of the north, spirit of earth,
of nighttime and winter:
Be with us in the darkness,
in the time of gestation.

A Prayer

Place your mind before the mirror of eternity!
Place your soul in the brilliance of glory!
Place your heart in the figure of the divine substance!
And transform your whole being into the image of the
Godhead Itself through contemplation!
So that you too may feel what His friends feel
As they taste the hidden sweetness
Which God Himself has reserved
From the beginning
For those who love Him.

Saint Clare of Assisi

Prayer of Affirmation

I would be true for there are those who trust me.
I would be pure for there are those who care.
I would be strong for there is much to suffer.
I would be brave for there is much to dare.
I would be friend of all, the foe, the friendless.
I would be forgiving and then forget the gift.
I would be humble for I know my weakness.
I would look up, and laugh, and love, and live.

Anonymous

Him to whom you pray is nearer to you
   than the neck of your camel.

Muhammad

Let me not pray to be sheltered from dangers,
But to be fearless in facing them.
Let me not beg for the stilling of my pain,
But for the heart to conquer it. Let me not look for allies
   in life's battlefield,
But to my own strength.
Let me not crave in anxious fear to be saved,
But hope for the patience to win my freedom.
Grant me that I may not be a coward, feeling your mercy
   in my success alone;
But let me find the grasp of your hand in my failure.

   Rabindranath Tagore

A Sufi Prayer

Know the world from end to end is a mirror;
In each atom a hundred stars are concealed.
If you pierce the heart of a single drop of water,
From it will flow a hundred dear oceans;
If you look intently at each speck of dust,
In it you will see a thousand beings;
A gnat in its lines is like an elephant;
In name a drop of water resembles the Nile,
In the heart of a barley-corn is stored a hundred harvests,
Within a millet-seed a world exists.
In an insect's wing is an ocean of life,
A heaven is concealed in the pupil of an eye,
The core in the center of the heart is small,
Yet the Lord of both worlds will enter there.

Mahmud ash-Shabisfari

Prayer for Assistance

O Lord, my God and my Haven in distress! My Shield and my Shelter in my woes! My Asylum and Refuge in time of need and in my loneliness my Companion! In my anguish my Solace, and in my solitude a loving Friend! The Remover of the pangs of my sorrows and the Pardoner of my sins!

Wholly unto Thee do I turn, fervently imploring Thee with all my heart, my mind and my tongue, to shield me from all that runs counter to Thy will in this, the cycle of Thy divine unity, and to cleanse me of all defilement that will hinder me from seeking, stainless and unsullied, the shade of the tree of Thy Grace.

Have mercy, O Lord, on the feeble, make whole the sick, and quench the burning thirst.

Gladden the bosom wherein the fire of Thy love doth smolder, and set it aglow with the flame of Thy celestial love and spirit.

Robe the tabernacles of divine unity with the vesture of holiness, and set upon my head the crown of Thy favor.

Illumine my face with the radiance of the orb of Thy bounty, and graciously aid me in ministering at Thy holy threshold.

Make my heart overflow with love for Thy creatures and grant that I may become the sign of Thy mercy, the token of Thy grace, the promoter of concord amongst Thy loved ones, devoted unto Thee, uttering Thy commemoration and forgetful of self but ever mindful of what is Thine.

O God, my God! Stay not from me the gentle gales of Thy pardon and grace, and deprive me not of the wellsprings of Thine aid and favor.

'Neath the shade of Thy protecting wings let me nestle, and cast upon me the glance of Thine all-protecting eye.

Loose my tongue to laud Thy name amidst Thy people, that my voice may be raised in great assemblies and from my lips may stream the flood of Thy praise.

Thou art, in all truth, the Gracious, the Glorified, the Mighty, the Omnipotent.

'Abdu'l-Bahá

Psalm 23

The Lord is my shepherd;
I shall not want.
He makes me lie down in green pastures;
He leads me beside still waters.
He restores my soul.
He leads me in paths of righteousness
　　for his name's sake.
Even though I walk through the valley
　　of the shadow of death,
I will fear no evil;
For thou art with me;
Thy rod and thy staff, they comfort me.
Thou preparest a table before me
In the presence of mine enemies;
Thou annointest my head with oil,
My cup overflows.
Surely goodness and mercy shall follow me
All the days of my life;
And I shall dwell in the house of the Lord forever.

Breakfast Grace

Lord, as we now break the fast,
We thank you for the night safe passed.
Now grant safekeeping on our way,
Good cheer and strength and health all day.

Thomas Elwood

Breakfast Prayer

Father we thank thee for the night
And for the pleasant morning light.
For rest and food and loving care,
And all that makes the day so fair.
Help us to do the things we should
To be to others kind and good,
In all we do, in all we say,
To grow more loving every day.

Rebecca J. Weston

A Prayer

Lord, behold our family here assembled.
We thank you for this place in which we dwell,
for the love that unites us,
for the peace accorded us this day,
for the hope with which we expect the morrow;
for the health, the work, the food and the bright skies
That make our lives delightful;
For our friends in all parts of the earth. Amen.

Robert Louis Stevenson

Prayer for a Day Full of Blessings

O sun, as you rise in the east through God's leadership,
Wash away all the evils of which I have thought throughout
    the night.
Bless me, so that my enemies will not kill me and my family;
Guide me through hard work.
O God, give me mercy upon our children who are suffering:
Bring riches today as the sun rises;
Bring all fortunes to me today.

In Kenya the old men of the Abaluyia people say this morning
prayer, where the sun is a symbol of God's perpetual presence.

Prayer for Children

Your children are not your children,
They are the sons and daughters of Life's longing for itself.
They come through you but not from you,
And though they are with you, yet they belong not to you.
You may give them your love but not your thoughts.
For they have their own thoughts.
You may house their bodies but not their souls,
For their souls dwell in the house of tomorrow,
Which you cannot visit, not even in your dreams.
You may strive to be like them, but seek not
to make them like you.
For life goes not backward nor tarries with yesterday.
You are the bows from which your children
As living arrows are sent forth.
The archer sees the mark upon the path of the infinite,
And He bends you with His might
That His arrows may go swift and far.
Let your bending in the archer's hand be for gladness;
For even as He loves the arrow that flies,
So He loves the bow that is stable.

Kahlil Gibran

Prayer for Consciousness

I have thrown from me the whirling dance of mind
And stand now in the spirit's silence free;
Timeless and deathless beyond creature-kind,
The center of my own eternity.
My mind is hushed in a wide and endless light,
My heart a solitude of delight and peace,
My sense ensnared by touch and sound and sight,
My body a point in white infinities.
I am the one Being's sole immobile Bliss:
No one I am, I who am all that is.

Aurobindo Ghose

Prayer for Detachment

O Lord! Unto Thee I repair for refuge, and toward all Thy
   signs I set my heart.

O Lord! Whether traveling or at home, and in my
occupation or in my work, I place my whole trust in Thee.

Grant me then Thy sufficing help so as to make me
independent of all things. O Thou Who art unsurpassed in
Thy mercy!

Bestow upon me my portion, O Lord, as Thou pleasest,
and cause me to be satisfied with whatsoever Thou hast
ordained for me.

Thine is the absolute authority to command.

The Báb

How the Soul Speaks to God

Lord, you are my lover,
My longing,
My flowing stream,
My sun,
And I am your reflection.

Mechtild of Magdeburg. Translated by Oliver Davies.

Prayer for Forgiveness

Thou seest me, O my Lord, with my face turned towards the heaven of Thy bounty and the ocean of Thy favor, withdrawn from all else beside Thee. I ask of Thee, by the splendors of the Sun of Thy revelation on Sinai, and the effulgences of the Orb of Thy grace which shineth from the horizon of Thy Name, the Ever-Forgiving, to grant me Thy pardon and to have mercy upon me. Write down, then, for me with Thy pen of glory that which will exalt me through Thy Name in the world of creation. Aid me, O my Lord, to set myself towards Thee, and to hearken unto the voice of Thy loved ones, whom the powers of the earth have failed to weaken, and the dominion of the nations has been powerless to withhold from Thee, and who, advancing towards Thee have said: "God is our Lord, the Lord of all who are in heaven and all who are on earth."

Bahá'u'lláh

O, Love

O, love, O pure deep love, be here, be now
Be all; worlds dissolve into your stainless endless radiance,
Frail living leaves burn with you brighter than cold stars:
Make me your servant, your breath, your core.

Jalal al-Din Rumi

A Prayer for Guidance

Grant me, O Lord,
to know what I ought to know,
to love what I ought to love,
to praise what delights you most,
to value what is precious in your sight,
to hate what is offensive to you.
Do not allow me to judge according to the sight of my eyes,
nor to pass sentence according to the hearing of the ears
    of ignorant men;
but to discern with a true judgment between things visible
    and spiritual, and above all things, always to inquire
    what is the good pleasure of your will.

Saint Thomas á Kempis

God never changes;
Patient endurance
Attains to all things;
Who God possesses
In nothing is wanting;
Alone God suffices.

Saint Teresa of Avila

Irish Prayer

May there always be work for your hands to do
May your purse always hold a coin or two
May the sun always shine upon your window pane
May a rainbow be certain to follow each rain
May the hand of a friend always be near to you and
May God fill your heart with gladness to cheer you.

Khasi Unitarian Prayer

O God, root and source of body and soul, we ask for
boldness in confronting evil. When you are within us,
we have the power to countenance all that is untrue.
O Father and Mother of all humankind, may we redeem
our failings by the good work that we do. In the name
of the one, the only God.

Prayer for Knowledge

A journey of a thousand miles must begin with a single step.
The softest things in the world overcome the hardest things
   in the world.
Non-being penetrates that in which there is no space.
Through this I know the advantage of taking no action.
One may know the world without going out of doors.
One may see the way of Heaven without looking through
   the windows.
The further one goes, the less one knows.
Therefore the sage knows without going about,
Understands without seeing,
And accomplishes without any action.

   Lao-Tzu

The essence of knowledge is, having it, to apply it; not having
it, to confess your ignorance.

   Confucius

Prayer of Praise

God is One and alone, and none other exists with Him;
God is the One, the One who has made all things.

He is eternal and infinite; He has endured for
countless ages, and He shall endure to all eternity.

God is a spirit, a hidden spirit, the Spirit of spirits,
the Divine Spirit.

He is a mystery to His creatures, and no man knows
how to know Him. His names are innumerable; they are
manifold, and no one knows their number.

God has made the universe, and He has created all that
is in it. He has stretched out the heavens and founded the
earth. What His heart conceived came to pass straightway,
and when He had spoken His word came to pass, and it
shall endure forever.

The Egyptian Book of the Dead

What does it profit you that all the libraries of the world should be yours? Not knowledge but what one does with knowledge is your profit.

Sa'ib of Tabriz

A Hindu Prayer for Peace in All Things

The peace in the sky, the peace in the mid-air,
the peace on the earth, the peace in the waters,
the peace in the plants, the peace in the forest trees,
the peace in All Devas, the peace in Brahman,
the peace in all things,
the peace in peace—
may that peace come to me!

Prayer for Spiritual Qualities

O my Lord! Make Thy beauty to be my food, and Thy presence my drink, and Thy pleasure my hope, and praise of Thee my action, and remembrance of Thee my companion, and the power of Thy sovereignty my succorer, and Thy habitation my home, and my dwelling-place the seat Thou hast sanctified from the limitations imposed upon them who are shut out as by a veil from Thee.

Thou art, verily, the Almighty, the All-Glorious, the Most Powerful.

Bahá'u'lláh

Students' Morning Prayer

O Lord God, we humbly beseech thee to direct our thoughts and prayers this day; purify our hearts from every evil and false imagination, and may no vain and worldly desires have their abode in us. Keep us from all wandering looks and ways, from an undevout mind, and careless prayers. Let the voice of thy love enter our souls, that we may study thy word with reverence and holy fear, with fervor and delight. O God, thou seest us: help us to look unto thee; for the sake of thy Son, Jesus Christ, our Lord. Amen.

The Office for Special Occasions, *Episcopalian Collection*

This prayer, which dates from about 1900, has been inspired by the sixteenth-century Anglican Book of Common Prayer.

Universal Tolerance

My heart is capable of every form,
a cloister of the monk, a temple for idols,
a pasture for gazelles, the votary's Ka'ba,
the tables of the Torah, the Qu'ran.
Love is the creed I hold: wherever turn
His camels, love is still my creed and faith.

Ibn 'Arabi

This personal creed of Ibn 'Arabi, the Sufi mystic, defines the Sufi
ideal of universal tolerance for all religious traditions: Christian,
polytheist, animist, Islamic, and Jewish.

Prayer to the Unity of All Life

Now under the loving kindness and care of the Buddha,
each believer of religion in the world transcends the
differences of religion, race, and nationality, discards small
differences, and unites in oneness to discuss sincerely how
to annihilate strife from the earth, how to reconstruct
a world without arms, and how to build the welfare and peace
of mankind, so that never-ending light and happiness can
be obtained for the world of the future.

> *From* Prayer: Language of the Soul
> *compiled by Philip Dunn*

Why do you go to the forest in search of the Divine? God lives
in all, and abides with you too. As fragrance dwells in a flower,
or reflection in a mirror, so the Divine dwells inside everything;
seek therefore in your own heart.

> *Tegh Bahadur*

Prayer of Welcome

My heart is filled with joy when I see you here, as the brooks fill with water when the snows melt in the spring, and I feel glad, as the ponies are when the fresh grass starts in the beginning of the year.

I heard of your coming, when I was many sleeps away, and I made but few camps before I met you. I knew that you had come to do good to me and to my people. I look for the benefits, which would last forever, and so my face shines with joy, as I look upon you.

Ten Bears

O Burning Mountain

O burning mountain, O chosen sun,
O perfect moon, O fathomless well,
O unattainable height, O clearness beyond measure,
O wisdom without end, O mercy without limit,
O strength beyond resistance, O crown of all majesty,
The humblest you created sings your praise.

Mechtild of Magdeburg

Every Creature Is a Book about God

Apprehend God in all things,
For God is in all things.
Every single creature is full of God
And is a book about God.
Every creature is a word of God.

If I spent enough time with the tiniest creature—
Even a caterpillar—
I would never have to prepare a sermon.
So full of God
Is every being.

    Meister Eckhart

Prayer for Work

Each morning I offer my body, my mind, and any ability that I
possess, to be used by Thee, O Infinite Creator, in whatever way
Thou dost choose to express Thyself through me. I know that
all work is Thy work, and that no task is too difficult or too menial
when offered to Thee in loving service.

    Paramahansa Yogananda

O God, Thou art more friend to me
than I am to myself.
I dedicate myself to Thee,
O Lord.

    'Abdu'l-Bahá

A Prayer

May thy peace and serenity bless us and the light of thy countenance shine upon our pathway henceforth and forever. In the silence may we feel the holy presence of God, our Creator. We open our hearts to the incoming of the light of God, praying that we may feel the impress of God's love drawing us all together in one spirit—those who are in the physical body, and the hosts in the world unseen.

We pray that we may realize this at-one-ment of spirit, and that during this service thy love may rise within our hearts and go out to all mankind, to all creation.

O gracious Spirit, we thank thee in humility for the expanding consciousness of thy goodness, thy love, in our hearts; and we thank thee for the knowledge of thy love and thy power to permeate our lives and lift them to thy world of beauty.

White Eagle

Yearning and Love for God

This day is dear to me above all other days, for today the
Beloved Lord is a guest in my house;
My chamber and my courtyard are beautiful with
    His presence;
My songs sing His Name, and they are become lost in His
Great Beauty: I wash His feet, and I look upon His Face and I
Lay before Him as a man offering my body, my mind, and all
    that I have.
What a day of gladness is that day in which my Beloved,
Who is my treasure, comes to my house. All evils fly from
My heart when I see my Lord.
My love has touched Him;
My heart is longing for the Name which is Truth.

Kabir

A Prayer from Babette's Feast

Oh, watch the day
Once again hurry off.
And the sun bathe
Itself in the water.
The time for us to rest approaches,
O God, who dwelleth in heavenly light,
Who reigns above in heaven's hall.
Be for us our infinite light
In the alley of the night.
The sand in our hourglass will soon run out.
The day is conquered by the night.
The glares of the world are ending,
So brief their day, so swift their flight.
God, let thy brightness ever shine.
Admit us to thy mercy divine.

Benediction

Throughout all generations
   we will render thanks unto Thee
And declare Thy praise,
Evening, morning, and noon,
For our lives which are in Thy care,
For our souls which are in Thy keeping,
For Thy miracles which we witness daily,
And for Thy wondrous deeds and blessings
   toward us at all times.

   The Kaddish

PART 2

UNIVERSAL SPIRITUAL SONGS

THE TRADITIONAL spiritual disciplines of prayer, meditation, and mindful singing may often be useful in cultivating a growing awareness of a person's inner life. Throughout the ages the human heart has lifted its voice in the majesty of spiritual expression through music and song. In the form of a soulful prayer, the spiritual song can acknowledge the presence of the Creator of all Creation. In praise and blessing the hymn can celebrate abundant harvest. A hymn can also capture the joy and the ecstasy of Spirit and bring jubilance to the singer!

The singing of hymns is a part of our heritage and a common experience in many communities through the world. In universal spiritual songs one can often find a potpourri of history, biography, and music in a devotional setting. Since the time of the great English composers, sacred music has expanded to include the singing of spirituals, gospels, and the modern praise songs that are so popular today.

For many centuries, in worship services throughout the world, the strains of hymns, spiritual songs, and contemporary music have offered celebration, leaving their mark on sacred music. And all kinds of music apply—both sacred and secular. The central focus of spiritual songs is often the worship and adoration of God. For many people, whom they are today may partially result from the blending of our spiritual inheritance and our God-given human heritage.

The ministry of music is important to our spiritual lives. Spiritual songs can help us recapture a sense of the sacred in the things we do every day of our lives—at home, at work, in the community, and in our personal and business relationships. Perhaps the words of the traditional song, "This Is the Day That the Lord Has Made," may bring a pause for thought awareness of the role the spiritual song may play in daily living.

> This is the day that the Lord has made,
> Let us rejoice and be glad in it.
> This is the day; this is the day
> That the Lord has made.

Hymn of Origins

In the beginning there was neither existence
    nor non-existence;
Neither the world nor the sky beyond.
What was covered over? Where? What gave it protection?
Was there water deep and unfathomable?

Then was neither death nor immortality,
Nor any sign of day or night,
That One breathed, without breath, by its own impulse;
Other than That there was nothing at all . . .

In the beginning was love,
Which was the primal germ of the mind.
The seers searching in their hearts with wisdom
Discovered the connection between existence
    and non-existence . . .

The Gods are later than this world's creation—
Therefore who knows from whence it came?
That out of which creation came,
Whether it held it together or did not,
He who sees it in the highest heaven,
He only knows—or perhaps even He does not know.

This hymn, over 3,000 years old, demonstrates the existence
of philosophical speculation.

Hymn to the Creator

The earth is full of your goodness,
your greatness and understanding,
your wisdom and harmony.
How wonderful
are the lights that you created.
You formed them
with strength and power
and they shine very wonderfully on the world,
magnificent in their splendour.
They arise in radiance
and go down in joy.
Reverently
they fulfill your divine will.
They are tributes to your name
as they exalt your sovereign rule
in song.

This is a Jewish hymn from the time of the Second Temple,
c. 516 B.C.–A.D.70

Gnostic Hymn from Nag Hammadi

Holy is God the Father of all, who is before the first beginning;
Holy is God, whose purpose is accomplished by his several
   powers;
Holy is God, who wills to be known, and is known by them
   that are his own.
     Holy art thou, who by thy word hast constructed all that is;
holy art thou, whose brightness nature has not darkened;
holy are thou, of whom all nature is an image.
     holy art thou, who art stronger than all domination;
holy art thou, who art greater than all preeminence;
holy art thou, who surpassest all praises.
     Accept pure offerings of speech from a soul and heart
       uplifted to thee, thou of whom no words can tell,
         no tongue can speak, whom silence only can declare.

Corpus Hermeticum

I Am God's Melody of Life

I am God's melody of life,
He sings His song through me.
I am God's rhythm and harmony,
He sings His song through me.
A song of life, of radiant life,
Of life so full and free.
I am God's melody of life,
He sings His song through me.
He sings His song through me.
He sings His song through me.

Georgiana Tree West

I'll Walk with God

I'll walk with God
From this day on.
His helping hand
I'll lean upon.
This is my prayer,
My humble plea
May the Lord be ever with me.
There is no death
Tho' eyes grow dim.
There is no fear
When I'm near to Him.
I'll lean on Him forever
And He'll forsake me never.
He will not fail me as long
As my faith is strong.
Whatever road I may walk along
I'll walk with God.
I'll take His hand.
I'll talk with God,
He'll understand.
I'll pray to Him, each day to Him
And He'll hear the word that I say.
His hand will guide my throne and rod,
And I'll never walk alone
While I walk with God!

Nikolaus Brodszky and Paul Francis Webster

Come into the Silence

Come into the silence,
Rest for a while.
Release all the cares of your day.
Come into the silence,
Quiet your mind.
Spirit has something to say.

If you will trust the Lord to guide you,
Trust the Lord beside you,
Be ye not afraid to let go.
Spirit will befriend you,
Spirit is within you.
Spirit is love, you know!

Nancy Abercrombie

Early Hymn from Orthodox Traditions

May none of God's wonderful works
keep silence, night or morning.
Bright stars, high mountains, the depths of the seas,
sources of rushing rivers:
may all these break into song as we sing
to Father, Son, and Holy Spirit.
May all the angels in the heavens reply:
Amen! Amen! Amen!
Power, praise, honor, eternal glory
to God, the only giver of grace.
Amen! Amen! Amen!

Oxyrhynchus Papyrus

Hymn to Perfect Wisdom

Homage to Thee, Perfect Wisdom,
Boundless and transcending thought!
All Thy limbs are without blemish,
Faultless those who Thee discern.

Spotless, unobstructed, silent,
Like the vast expanse of space;
Who in truth does really see Thee
The Tathagata perceives.

As the moonlight does not differ
From the moon, so also Thou
Who aboundest in holy virtues,
And the Teacher of the world.

Those, all pity, who came to Thee,
Buddha–dharmas heralding,
They will win with ease, O Gracious!
Majesty beyond compare.

This is an excerpt from a long hymn to Buddha.

Shaker Funeral Hymn

Our sister's gone, she is no more;
She's quit our coast, she's left our shore;
She's burst the bounds of mortal clay,
The spirit's fled and soars away.
We now may hear the solemn call:
"Be ye prepared, both great and small."
The call excludes no sex or age,
For all must quit this mortal stage.
Then let the righteous sing,
When from corruption they get free:
O death where is thy sting?
O grave where is thy victory?

The Hymn Eternal

Shaker; from Canterbury, NH
HYFRYDOL 8.7.8.7.D.
Rowland H. Prichard (1811–1887); arr. Ralph Vaughan Williams (1872–1958)

1. There are notes of joy and beau - ty In my psalm of
2. From my theme of Chris - tian du - ty, Rich in ca - den -

praise to - day; There are chords of peace and bless - ing, Sweet - ly
ces of peace, Rise full meas - ures keyed to tri - umph, As the

blend-ing all the way. I will add no strain of dis - cord,
tones of trust in - crease. Heav'n-ly mel - o - dies I'm sing - ing,

But at - tune my voice to prayer, Giv - ing heart and
U - ni - son with powers on high, Syl - la - bled the

hand in ser - vice, Sing my psalm with trust and care.
hymn e - ter - nal, In the love that can - not die.

It Sounds Along the Ages
William Channing Gannett (1840–1923)
LANCASHIRE 7.6.7.6.D.
Henry Smart (1813–1879)

1. It sounds a-long the a-ges, soul an-swer-ing to soul; it
2. From Si-nai's cliffs it ech-oed, it breathed from Bud-dha's tree, it
3. It calls—and lo, new jus-tice! It speaks—and lo, new truth! In

kin-dles on the pag-es of ev-ery Bi-ble scroll; the
charmed in Ath-ens' mar-ket, it hal-lowed Gal-i-lee; the
ev-er no-bler stat-ure and un-ex-haust-ed youth. For-

psalm-ist heard and sang it, from mar-tyr lips it broke, and
ham-mer stroke of Lu-ther, the Pil-grims' sea-side prayer, the
ev-er on re-sound-ing, and know-ing nought of time, our

proph-et tongues out-rang it till sleep-ing na-tions woke.
or-a-cles of Con-cord one ho-ly word de-clare.
laws but catch the mu-sic of its e-ter-nal chime.

Simple Gifts

Words and music by Elder Joseph Brackett, 1797–1882
ed.& arr. Robert A.M. Ross (b.1955), from a facsimile of a Shaker manuscript

'Tis the gift to be sim-ple, 'tis the gift to be free, 'Tis the gift to come down where we ought to be. And when we find our-selves in the place just right 'Twill be in the val-ley of love and de-light. When true sim-pli-ci-ty is gain'd To bow and to bend we shan't be a-sham'd; To turn, turn will be our de-light Till by turn-ing, turn-ing we come round right.

Hymn of Saint Gregory the Great

Attr. Gregory the Great (c.540–604); trans. unknown
TALLIS' CANON L.M.
Thomas Tallis (c.1505–1585)

1. Di - vine cre - a - tor of the light, Who, bring - ing forth the gold - en ray, Didst join the morn - ing with the night And call the bless - ed un - ion day;

2. We bow to thee, whose might - y word Made time be - gin and hea - ven move; Hear thou our tear - ful prayer, O Lord, And warm us with the light of love.

3. Lord, let no crime our souls op - press, Or keep us from thy law di - vine; Oh, guard us by thy sav - ing grace And make our wills ac - cord with thine.

4. Still may we seek thy heaven - ly seat, And strive e - ter - nal life to gain; Oh, keep us in thy mer - cy sweet, And cleanse our souls from earth - ly stain.

On Eagle's Wings

Michael Joncas (b.1951); after Psalm 91
Music by Michael Joncas

1. You who dwell in the shel-ter of the Lord, Who a-bide in His shad-ow for life, Say to the Lord, "My ref - uge, My rock in whom I trust!"

Refrain:

And He will raise you up on ea - gle's wings, Bear you on the breath of dawn, Make you to shine like the sun, And hold you in the palm of His hand.

(To Verses; last time to Coda)

Verse 2:

2. The snare of the fowl-er will nev-er cap-ture you, And fam-ine will bring you no fear: Un-der His wings your ref - uge, His faith-ful - ness, your shield.

To Refrain

Verse 3:

3. You need not fear the ter-ror of the night, Nor the ar-row that flies by day. Though thou-sands fall a-bout you, Near you it shall not come.

To Refrain

Verse 4:

4. For to His an-gels He's giv-en a com-mand To

guard you in all of your ways; Up - on their hands they will

bear you up, Lest you dash your foot a - gainst a stone.

To Refrain

Hymn to the Night

Henry Wadsworth Longfellow (1807–1882)
NOCTURNE 10.6.10.6.
Robert A.M. Ross (b.1955)

1. I heard the trail-ing gar-ments of the Night Sweep
2. I felt her pres-ence, by its spell of might, Stoop
3. I heard the sounds of sor-row and de-light, The
4. From the cool cis-terns of the mid-night air My
5. O ho-ly Night! from thee I learn to bear What
(Slower) 6. Peace! Peace! O-res-tes-like I breathe this prayer! De-

through her mar - ble halls! I
o'er me from a - bove; The
man - i - fold, soft chimes, That
spir - it drank re - pose; The
man has borne be - fore! Thou
scend with broad - winged flight, The

saw her sa - ble skirts all fringed with light
calm, ma - jes - tic pres - ence of the Night,
fill the haunt-ed cham-bers of the Night,
foun - tain of per - pe - tual peace flows there,
layest thy fin - ger on the lips of Care,
wel - come, the thrice-prayed for, the most fair,

From the ce - les - tial   walls!
As   of the one   I   love.
Like some old po - et's   rhymes.
From those deep cis - terns   flows.
And they com-plain no   more.

The   best - be - lov - èd Night!

Universal Love
Shaker; from Canterbury, NH

1. Blest be that u-ni-ver-sal love For which the Chris-tian aims; Whose
2. Be lift-ed up, O vir-gin throng, With o-pen hearts em-brace The
3. Its re-al sub-jects grand-ly rise Su-pe-rior in their sway O'er

source in God is found a-bove All nar-row hu-man claims. As
prin-ci-ple which pu-ri-fies And el-e-vates the race. The
earth-ly loves and ten-den-cies, In ac-tion, word and way. Then

tow'rs the loft-y moun-tain top A-bove the dis-tant sea, So
love which seeks the good of all, In ev'-ry land and clime, Which
let us join this no-ble band And seek the joy, the hope, The

stand the mer-its of this love In its di-vin-i-ty.
vi-tal-i-zes, cheers, for-gives, And ren-ders life sub-lime.
free-dom which this love will bring, Found al-ways "High-er up."

Be Thou My Vision

Ancient Irish; trans. Mary E. Byrne (1880–1931); versified by Eleanor H. Hull (1860–1935); alt.
SLANE 10.10.9.10.
Traditional Irish Melody; harm. Carlton R. Young (b.1926)

1. Be thou my vi - sion, O God of my heart,
2. Be thou my wis - dom, and thou my true word,
3. Rich - es I heed not, nor world's emp - ty praise,

naught be all else to me, save that thou art.
I ev - er with thee and thou with me God;
thou my in - her - i - tance, now and al - ways;

Thou my best thought, by day or by night,
thou my soul's shel - ter, thou my high tower,
thou and thou on - ly, first in my heart,

wak- ing or sleep - ing, thy pres - ence my light.
raise thou me heaven - ward, O Power of my power.
Sov - 'reign of heav - en, my trea - sure thou art.

God of the Earth, the Sky, the Sea

Samuel Longfellow (1819–1892)
DUKE STREET L.M.
John Hatton (1710–1793)

1. God of the earth, the sky, the sea,
2. Your love is in the sun - shine's glow,
3. We feel your calm at eve - ning's hour,
4. But high - er far, and far more clear,

mak - er of all a - bove, be - low,
your life is in the quick - 'ning air;
your gran-deur in the march of night;
you in our spir - it we be - hold;

cre - a - tion lives and moves in you;
when light-nings flash and storm - winds blow,
and when the morn - ing breaks in power,
your im - age and your - self are there—

your pres - ent life through all does flow.
there is your power, your law is there.
we hear your word, "Let there be light."
in - dwell-ing God, pro - claimed of old.

Mysterious Presence, Source of All

Seth Curtis Beach (1837–1932)
WAREHAM L.M.
William Knapp (1698–1768)

1. Mys - te - rious Pres - ence, source of all— the
2. Thou breath - est in the rush - ing wind, thy
3. Thy hand un - seen to ac - cents clear a -
4. That touch di - vine a - gain im - part, still

world with - out, the soul with - in— thou
spir - it stirs in leaf and flower; nor
woke the psalm - ist's trem - bling lyre, and
give the proph - et's burn - ing word; and

fount of life, O hear our call, and
wilt thou from the will - ing mind with -
touched the lips of ho - ly seer with
vo - cal in each wait - ing heart let

pour thy liv - ing wa - ters in.
hold thy light and love and power.
flame from thine own al - tar fire.
liv - ing psalms of praise be heard.

O, the Beauty in a Life

Based on a text by Bishop Toribio Quimada
QUIMADA Irregular
Traditional Visayan (Filipino) folk tune; arr. Robert A.M. Ross (b.1955)

1. O, the beau - ty in a life that il-lu - mines hon - or a - new, that mod - els wise and gra - cious ways to ev - ery seek - - - - - -
2. Let not ser - vice of the good be con-fined to great saints a-lone, but ev - ery hour be part of all our dai - ly liv - - - - - -
3. O, the beau - ty of a life that il-lu - mines care of the soul, that knows a love that is for self as well as oth - - - - - -

Let Love Continue Long

Berkley L. Moore (b. 1932)
LOVE UNKNOWN 6.6.6.6.8.8.
John Ireland (1879–1962)

Unison

1. Let love con-tin-ue long, and show to us the way, and if that love be strong, no hurt can have a say; and if that love re-main but strong, no hurt can ev-er have a say.

2. If love can-not be found, though com-mon faith pre-vails, when love does not a-bound, a com-mon faith will fail. When hu-man love does not a-bound, a com-mon faith will al-ways fail.

3. If we in love u-nite, de-bate can cause no strife: for with this love in sight, dis-putes en-rich our life. For with this bond of hu-man love, dis-putes can mean a rich-er life.

4. May love con-tin-ue long, and lead us on our way: for if that love be strong, no hurt can have a say. For if that love re-main but strong, no hurt can ev-er have a say.

O God, Our Help in Ages Past

Isaac Watts (1674–1748); paraphrase of Psalm 90
ST. ANNE C.M.
William Croft (1678–1727)

1. O God, our help in a - ges past, our
2. Be - fore the hills in or - der stood, or
3. A thou - sand a - ges in thy sight are
4. Time, like an ev - er - roll - ing stream, soon
5. O God, our help in a - ges past, our

hope for years to come, our shel - ter from the
earth re - ceived its frame, from ev - er - last - ing
like an eve - ning gone, short as the watch that
bears us all a - way: we fly for - got - ten,
hope for years to come, be thou our guard while

storm - y blast, and our e - ter - nal home.
thou art God, to end - less years the same.
ends the night be - fore the ris - ing sun.
as a dream dies at the open - ing day.
trou - bles last, and our e - ter - nal home.

Creative Love, Our Thanks We Give

William DeWitt Hyde (1858–1917); adapt. Beth Ide (b.1921)
TRUTH FROM ABOVE L.M.
English melody; harm. Ralph Vaughan Williams (1872–1958)

1. Cre - a - tive love, our thanks we give that
2. That we are not yet ful - ly wise, that
3. What though the fu - ture long de - lay, and
4. Since what we choose is what we are, and

this, our world, is in - com - plete, that
we are in the mak - ing still— as
still with faults we dai - ly cope? It
what we love we yet shall be, the

strug - gle greets our will to live, that
friends who share one en - ter - prise and
gives us that for which to pray, a
goal may ev - er shine a - far— The

work a - waits our hands and feet;
strive to blend with na - ture's will.
field for toil and faith and hope.
will to reach it makes us free.

Children of the Human Race

John Andrew Storey (b.1935)
SERVETUS 7.7.7.7.D.
Thomas Oboe Lee (b.1945)

1. Chil - dren of the hu-man race, off-spring of our Moth-er Earth,
2. Should some sigh of oth-ers reach this, our lone-ly plan-et Earth,

not a-lone in end-less space has our plan-et giv-en birth.
dif-feren-ces of form and speech must not hide our com-mon worth.

Far a-cross the cos-mic skies count-less suns in glo-ry blaze,
When at length our minds are free, and the clouds of fear dis-perse,

and from un-told plan-ets rise end-less can-ti-cles of praise.
then at last we'll learn to be Chil-dren of the U-ni-verse.

We Would Be One

Samuel Anthony Wright (b.1919)
FINALNDIA 11.10.11.10.11.10.
Jean Sibelius (1865–1957); arr. from The Hymnal, *1933*

1. We would be one as now we join in sing - ing
2. We would be one in build-ing for to - mor - row

our hymn of love, to pledge our - selves a - new
a no - bler world than we have known to - day.

to that high cause of great - er un - der - stand-ing
We would be one in search-ing for that mean - ing

of who we are, and what in us is true.
which binds our hearts and points us on our way.

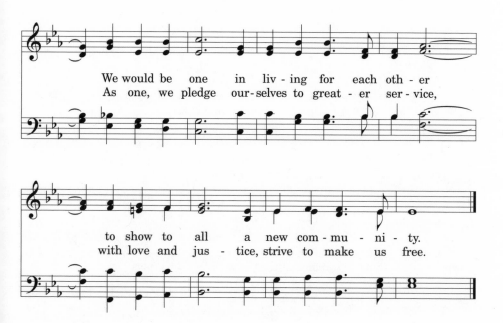

We would be one   in liv - ing for   each oth - er
As one, we pledge   our-selves to great - er   ser - vice,

to show to   all   a new com - mu - ni - ty.
with love and   jus - tice, strive to make   us   free.

Life Is the Greatest Gift of All

William E. Oliver; adapt. Waldemar Hillem (b. 1908)
BROTHER JAMES' AIR 8.6.8.6.8.6.
James Leith McBeth Bain (c.1840–1925); arr. David Dawson (b.1939)

Unison

1. Life is the great-est gift of all the rich-es on this earth; life and its crea-tures, great and small, of high and low - ly birth; so trea-sure it and mea-sure it with deeds of shin - ing worth.

2. Mind is the bright-est gift of all, its thought no bar - rier mars; it seeks cre-a - tion's hid - den plan, its quest sur-mounts all bars; it reins the wind, it chains the storm, it weighs the out - most stars.

3. We are of life, its shin-ing gift, the meas-ure of all things; up from the dust our tem-ples lift, our vi - sion soars on wings; for seed and root, for flower and fruit, our grate - ful spir - it sings.

All People That on Earth Do Dwell

William Kethe (d. 1608); recast by Alicia S. Carpenter (b. 1930)
OLD HUNDREDTH L.M.
Genevan Psalter, *1551*

1. All peo - ple that on earth do dwell,
2. O wel - come in this day with praise;
3. For we be - lieve that life is good,

sing ye a - loud with cheer - ful voice;
ap - proach with joy your God un - to;
love doth a - bide for - ev - er - more;

let hearts in ex - ul - ta - tion swell;
give thanks, and faith pro - claim al - ways,
truth, firm - er than a rock hath stood,

come now to - geth - er and re - joice.
for it is seem - ly so to do.
and shall from age to age en - dure.

Love Divine

Charles Wesley (1707–1788)
BEECHER 8.7.8.7.D.
John Zundel (1815–1882)

1. Love di - vine, all love ex - cel - ling, Joy of heav'n to
2. Breathe, oh, breathe Thy lov - ing Spir - it In - to ev - 'ry
3. Come, Al - might - y to de - liv - er! Let us all Thy
4. Fin - ish, then, Thy new cre - a - tion, Pure, un - spot - ted

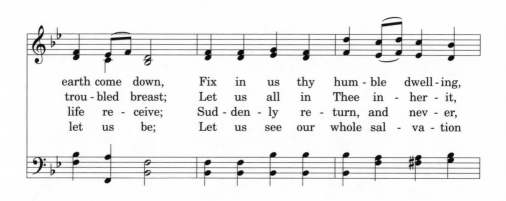

earth come down, Fix in us thy hum - ble dwell - ing,
trou - bled breast; Let us all in Thee in - her - it,
life re - ceive; Sud - den - ly re - turn, and nev - er,
let us be; Let us see our whole sal - va - tion

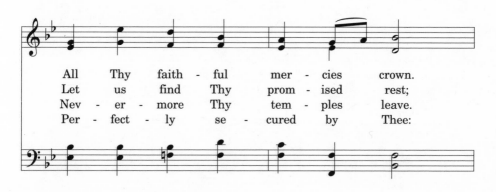

All Thy faith - ful mer - cies crown.
Let us find Thy prom - ised rest;
Nev - er - more Thy tem - ples leave.
Per - fect - ly se - cured by Thee:

Je - sus, Thou art all com - pas - sion, Pure, un - bound - ed
Take a - way the love of sin - ning, Al - pha and O -
Thee we would be al - ways bless - ing; Serve Thee as Thy
Changed from glo - ry in - to glo - ry Till in heav'n we

love Thou art; Vis - it us with Thy sal - va - tion,
me - ga be; End of faith, as its be - gin - ning,
hosts a - bove; Pray, and praise Thee with - out ceas - ing;
take our place— Till we cast our crowns be - fore Thee,

En - ter ev - 'ry trem - bling heart.
Set our hearts at lib - er - ty.
Glo - ry in Thy per - fect love.
Lost in won - der, love, and praise.

Sweet Hour of Prayer
William W. Walford (1772–1850)
SWEET HOUR 8.8.8.8.D.
William B. Bradbury (1816–1868)

1. Sweet hour of prayer, sweet hour of prayer, That calls me
2. Sweet hour of prayer, sweet hour of prayer, Thy wings shall
3. Sweet hour of prayer, sweet hour of prayer, May I thy

from a world of care, And bids me, at my
my pe - ti - tion bear To Him, whose truth and
con - so - la - tion share, Till, from Mount Pis - gah's

Fa - ther's throne, Make all my wants and wish - es
faith - ful - ness En - gage the wait - ing soul to
loft - y height, I view my home, and take my

known! In sea - sons of dis - tress and grief, My
bless: And since He bids me seek His face, Be -
flight: This robe of flesh I'll drop, and rise, To

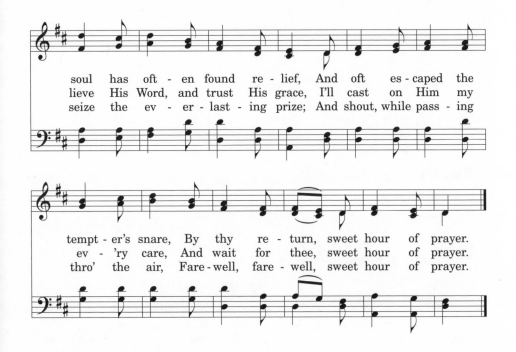

soul has oft - en found re - lief, And oft es - caped the
lieve His Word, and trust His grace, I'll cast on Him my
seize the ev - er - last - ing prize; And shout, while pass - ing

tempt - er's snare, By thy re - turn, sweet hour of prayer.
ev - 'ry care, And wait for thee, sweet hour of prayer.
thro' the air, Fare - well, fare - well, sweet hour of prayer.

O God, Thy Power Is Wonderful

Frederick W. Faber (1814–1863)
BEATITUDO C.M.
John B. Dykes (1823–1876)

1. O God, Thy pow'r is won - der - ful, Thy glo - ry pass - ing bright; Thy wis - dom with its deep on deep, A rap - ture to the sight.
2. I see Thee in th'e - ter - nal years In glo - ry all a - lone, Ere round Thine un - cre - a - ted fires Cre - a - ted light had shone.
3. I see Thee walk in E - den's shade, I see Thee all thro' time; Thy pa - tience and com - pas - sion seem New at - tri - butes sub - lime.
4. I see Thee when the doom is o'er, And out-worn time is done, Still, still in - com - pre - hen - si - ble, O God, yet not a - lone.
5. O lit - tle heart of mine! shall pain Or sor - row make thee moan, When all this God is all for thee, A Fa - ther all thine own?

Soul Questioning

Shaker; from Canterbury, NH

It comes to me in still hours As I thought-ful-ly, care-ful-ly muse, Where un-to are giv-en the powers That God hath as-signed me to use. Thro' faith I'm sure of His jus-tice As sow-ing, the reap-ing is mine; O Lord, grant Thy guid-ance so ho - ly That my will be sown with Thine.

My Psalm

Shaker; from Canterbury, NH

Pa - tient and faith - ful, yet joy - ful my soul,

Ask - ing in all things that wis - dom con - trol;

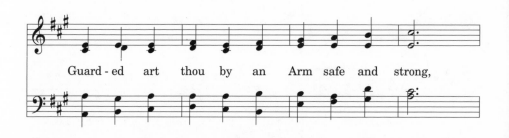

Guard - ed art thou by an Arm safe and strong,

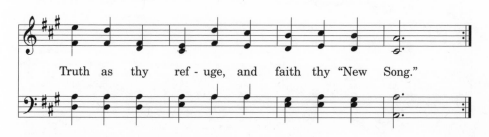

Truth as thy ref - uge, and faith thy "New Song."

Hal-lowed thy trust,— let its wings bear thee on To

heights grand - ly ris - ing as vic - t'ries are won.

Op - 'ning new pag - es of life, joy and peace, A

heav - en-crowned home tho' its meas-ures in - crease.

Daily Blessings
Shaker; from Canterbury, NH

As new ev-'ry morn-ing Thy mer-cies de-scend, And

bless-ings so rich crown each day, Free, free from the

fount of Thy good-ness I drink,— Thy truth is my

shield and my stay. My life ev-er guid-ed by

coun - sel di - vine, While strength for each du - ty is

giv'n, In glad - ness of heart my thanks-giv - ing as -

cends,— A sac - ri - fice new un - to heav'n.

Heaven's Blessing

Shaker; from Canterbury, NH

I will o-pen the win-dows of heav'n to thee And send forth a bless-ing di-vine, That will clothe thee with wis-dom and crown thee with peace, As mes-sen-gers will-ing of mine. In thy keep-ing are treas-ures of e-ter-nal wealth, Gifts need-ful for thee I pre-pare; Wher-ev-er thy mis-sion doth call thee to serve, My pres-ence shall go with thee there.

Willing Service
Shaker; from Canterbury, NH
BEACH SPRING 8.7.8.7.D.
The Sacred Harp, *1844; arr. Robert A.M. Ross (b.1955)*

1. In Thy wis-dom, Fa - ther, guide me In the way that seem-eth
2. When al - lur - ing paths have o - pened To be-guile the way-ward

best; Where-so - e'er I'm need-ed, choose me, To Thy
step, Thou hast in Thy lov - ing kind - ness An-gels

good - ness I'll at - test. In the bright - est, dark-est
sent to in - ter - cept. Hav-ing guid - ed thus far

hour Thou hast not for - sak - en me, For be -
safe - ly, Led me o - ver dang'- rous ways, Rec - og -

yond the gloom has ris - en Just suf - fi - cient light to see.
niz - ing Thy sure mer - cies, I would serve Thee all my days.

God's Love

Shaker; from Mt. Lebanon, NY
NETTLETON 8.7.8.7.D.
John Wyeth's Repository of Sacred Music, *1813*

1. O the love of God how pre-cious! Fill-ing all im-men-si-ty; And His mer-cy, O how bound-less, Last-ing as e-ter-ni-ty. Guid-ing us to per-fect heav-en, Where no e-vil can in-trude; May this love so free-ly giv-en, Fill our hearts with grat-i-tude.

2. By this love we're led to serve Him And to bear the chast'-ning rod; By this love we hope to tri-umph In o-be-dience to His word. Bless us with that ho-ly fer-vor, That shall quick-en us to be Sons and daugh-ters of His like-ness, By the truth made whol-ly free.

3. Gra-cious Fa-ther, we sur-ren-der Time and tal-ents, all we claim; Ask-ing to be wor-thy ev-er These to of-fer in Thy name. May Thy love pre-serve and hold us To a life di-vine-ly pure; Light the dark-est night, O Fa-ther, With Thy love a pass-port sure.

It Sounds Along the Ages
William Channing Gannett (1840–1923)
LANCASHIRE 7.6.7.6.D.
Henry Smart (1813–1879)

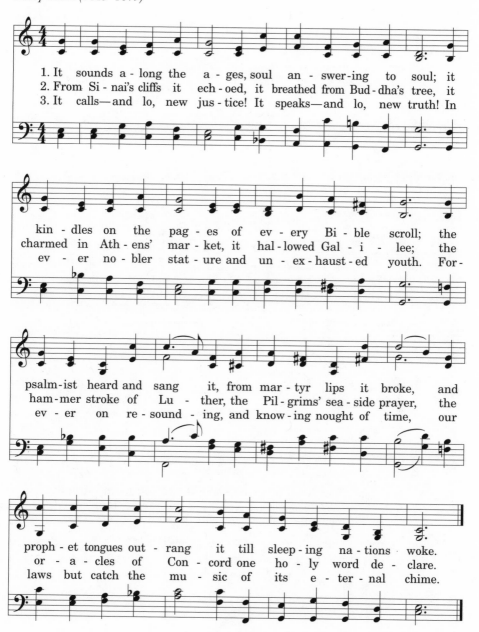

1. It sounds a - long the a - ges, soul an - swer-ing to soul; it
2. From Si - nai's cliffs it ech - oed, it breathed from Bud - dha's tree, it
3. It calls—and lo, new jus - tice! It speaks—and lo, new truth! In

kin - dles on the pag - es of ev - ery Bi - ble scroll; the
charmed in Ath - ens' mar - ket, it hal - lowed Gal - i - lee; the
ev - er no - bler stat - ure and un - ex - haust - ed youth. For-

psalm-ist heard and sang it, from mar - tyr lips it broke, and
ham-mer stroke of Lu - ther, the Pil - grims' sea - side prayer, the
ev - er on re - sound - ing, and know-ing nought of time, our

proph - et tongues out - rang it till sleep - ing na - tions woke.
or - a - cles of Con - cord one ho - ly word de - clare.
laws but catch the mu - sic of its e - ter - nal chime.

God of Many Names

Brian Wren (b.1936)
MANY NAMES 5.5.8.8. with refrain
William P. Rowan (b.1951)

1. God of man - y Names, gath - ered in - to One,
2. God of Jew - ish faith, Ex - o - dus and Law,
3. God of Wound - ed Hands, Web and Loom of love,

in your glo - ry come and meet us, Mov - ing, end - less - ly Be - com - ing;
in your glo - ry come and meet us, joy of Mir - i - am and Mo - ses;
in your glo - ry come and meet us, Car - pen - ter of new cre - a - tion;

God of Hov - ering Wings, Womb and Birth of time,
God of Je - sus Christ, Rab - bi of the poor,
God of man - y Names gath - ered in - to One,

joy - ful - ly we sing your prais - es, Breath of life in ev - ery peo - ple—
joy - ful - ly we sing your prais - es, cru - ci - fied, a - live for - ev - er—
joy - ful - ly we sing your prais - es, Mov - ing, end - less - ly Be - com - ing—

Hush, hush, hal - le - lu - ja, hal - le - lu - ja! Shout, shout, hal - le - lu - ja, hal - le - lu - ja!

Sing, sing, hal - le - lu - ja, hal - le - lu - ja! Sing God is love, God is love!

O God of Stars and Sunlight

John Holmes (1904–1962)
AURELIA 7.6.7.6.D.
Samuel Sebastian Wesley (1810–1876)

1. O God of stars and sun-light, whose wind lifts up a bird, in
2. O God of cloud and moun-tain, whose rain on rock is art, thy
3. O God of root and shad-ing of boughs a-bove our head; we

march-ing wave and leaf - fall we hear thy pa-tient word. The
plan and care and mean - ing re - new the head and heart. Thy
breathe in thy long breath - ing, our spir - it spir-it - ed. We

col - or of thy sea - sons goes gold a - cross the land: by
word and col - or spo - ken, thy sum - mer noons and showers by
walk be-neath thy bless - ing, thy sea - sons, and thy way, O

green up - on the tree - tops we know thy mov - ing hand.
these and by thy day - shine, we know thy world is ours.
God of stars and sun - light, O God of night and day.

Immortal, Invisible

Walter Chalmers Smith (1824–1908); based on 1 Timothy 1:17
ST. DENIS 11.11.11.11.
John Roberts's Caniadau y Cyssegr, 1839

1. Im - mor-tal, in - vis - i - ble, God on - ly wise. In
2. Un - rest-ing, un - hast-ing, and si - lent as night, nor
3. To all, life thou giv-est, to great and to small; in

light in - ac - ces - si - ble hid from our eyes, most
want-ing, nor was-ting, thou rul - est in might; thy
all life thou liv - est, the true life of all; all

bless - ed, most glo - rious, the An - cient of Days, al -
jus - tice like moun-tains high soar - ing a - bove thy
laud we would ren - der; oh, help us to see, 'tis

might - y, vic - to - rious, thy great name we praise.
clouds which are foun - tains of good - ness and love.
on - ly the splen - dor of light hid - eth thee.

Let the Whole Creation Cry

Stopford Augustus Brooke (1832–1916), based on Psalm 148
SALZBURG 7.7.7.7.D.
Jacob Hintze (1622–1702); harm. J.S. Bach (1685–1750); from Hymns Ancient and Modern, 1861

1. Let the whole cre - a - tion cry, "Glo - ry be to God on high!"
2. Chant in hon - or, o - cean fair; earth, soft rush-ing through the air;
3. You to whom the arts be - long, add your voic - es to the song;

Heaven and earth, a - wake and sing, to your God your prais - es bring.
birds, with morn and dew e - late, sing with joy at heav - en's gate.
bards of knowl-edge and of law, to the glo - rious cir - cle draw.

Sun and moon, up - lift your voice, night and stars, in God re - joice;
Let the blos-soms of the earth join the u - ni - ver-sal mirth;
From the north to south-ern pole let the might-y cho-rus roll:

sun-shine, dark-ness, cloud, and storm, rain and snow in praise per-form.
men and wom-en, young and old, raise the an-them man - i - fold.
"Ho - ly, ho - ly, ho - ly," cry; "Glo - ry be to God on high!"

Love Makes a Bridge

Brian Wren (b.1936)
CARITAS 4.8.4.8.
Robert A.M. Ross (b.1955)

1. Love makes a bridge from heart to heart, and
2. Love breaks the walls of lan-guage, gen - der,
3. Love lifts the hopes that force and fear have
4. Love rings the bells of want - ed birth and
5. Love makes a bridge that winds may shake, yet

hand to hand. Love finds a way, when
class, and age. Love gives us wings to
beat - en down. Love breaks the chains and
wed - ding day. Love guides the hands that
not de - stroy. Love car - ries faith through

laws are blind, and free - dom banned.
slip the bars of ev - ery cage.
gives us strength to stand our ground.
prom - ise more than words can say.
life and death, to end - less joy.

Press On

Shaker; from Canterbury, NH

1. Press on, on tri-um-phant-ly, The vic-to-ry is
2. Press on, on, tho' fears as-sail, Tho' rest-less doubts op-

sure to come; Tho' clouds oft ob-scure the day, Trust in God's al-
press thy soul; For God's love shall still pre-vail While e-ter-nal

might-y arm. He'll lead thee o'er the moun-tain high, And
a-ges roll. From threat-'ning foe He bids thee rise To

thro' the bar-ren plains of doubt; Will prove that He is
join the hosts of strength so near; His shield of faith will

ev-er nigh,— On sure ground He'll bring thee out.
guard the wise, Press on, on, be-yond all fear.

Take Time to Be Holy

William D. Longstaff (1822–1894)
HOLINESS 6.5.6.5.D.
George C. Stebbins (1846–1945)

1. Take time to be ho - ly, Speak oft with thy Lord;
2. Take time to be ho - ly, Be calm in thy soul,

A - bide in Him al - ways, And feed on His Word.
Each thought and each mo - tive Be - neath His con - trol;

Make friends of God's chil - dren, Help those who are weak,
Thus led by His Spir - it, Like Him thou shalt be;

For - get - ting in noth - ing His bless - ing to seek.
Thy friends in thy con - duct His like - ness shall see.

The Prayer of Faith

Hannah More Kohaus (1745–1833)
HURSLEY L.M.; adapted from GROSSER GOTT, WIR LOBEN DICH
Katholisches Gesangbuch, *Vienna, c.1774*

1. God is my help in ev - ery need;
2. I now am wise, I now am true,
3. God is my health, I can't be sick;

God does my ev - ery hun - ger feed;
Pa - tient, kind and lov - ing, too.
God is my strength, un - fail - ing, quick;

God walks be - side me, guides my way
All things I am, can do, and be,
God is my all, I know no fear,

Through ev - ery mo - ment of the day.
Through Christ, the Truth that is in me.
Since God and love and Truth are here.

We Gather Together

Netherlands folk hymn; trans. unknown
KREMSER *Irregular*
Adrian Valerius's Nederlandtsch Gedenkclanck, *1626; arr. Edward Kremser (1838–1914)*

1. We gath-er to-geth-er to ask the Lord's bless-ing, In
2. With-in us a-bid-ing, our God ev-er guid-ing, Or-
3. We come to sing prais-es with glad al-le-lu-ias, And

si-lence and ser-vice His will now is done. His
dain and main-tain Your true king-dom di-vine. As
know that in giv-ing our bless-ing shall be. Let

word ev-er stress-ing, His won - der ex-press-ing, Sing
from the be-gin-ning, the prize we are win-ning; O
this con-gre-ga-tion pro-claim the new cre-a-tion; In

prais - es to the Fa - ther, We know we are one!
Light, re-veal the way, O Love, in us shine!
Spir - it, we are one, In Christ, we are free!

Come, Ye Thankful People, Come

Henry Alford (1810–1871)
ST. GEORGE'S WINDSOR 7.7.7.7.D.
George Job Elvey (1816–1893)

1. Come, ye thank-ful peo - ple, come, Raise the song of har-vest home;
2. All the world is God's own field, Fruit un - to His praise to yield;
3. For the Lord our God shall come, And shall take His har-vest home;

All is safe - ly gath - ered in, Ere the win-ter storms be - gin;
Wheat and tares to - geth - er sown, Un - to joy or sor - row grown;
From His field shall in that day All of-fens-es purge a - way;

God, our Mak - er, doth pro - vide For our wants to be sup - plied;
First the blade, and then the ear, Then the full corn shall ap - pear;
There, for - ev - er pur - i - fied, In His pres-ence to a - bide,—

Come to God's own tem - ple, come. Raise the song of har - vest home.
Lord of har - vest, grant that we Whole - some grain and pure may be.
E - ven so, Lord, quick - ly come, Raise the glo - rious har - vest home.

When All the Peoples on This Earth

Anonymous
CHRISTMAS HYMN L.M.
Betty Jo Angebranndt (b.1931)

1. When all the peo - ples on this earth know deep in-
2. The choice to be the best we can be - gins the
3. The lights of Kwan - zaa now pro - claim that when we

side their pre - cious worth, when ev - ery sin - gle soul is
day we say, "I am." The u - ni - ty for which we
share our in - ner flame and nur - ture root and branch with

free, we'll earn the name Hu - man - i - ty.
sigh will nev - er come through hate or lie.
pride, we'll har - vest peace both far and wide.

Light of Ages and of Nations

Samuel Longfellow (1819–1892)
IN BABILONE 8.7.8.7.D.
Oude en nieuwe Hollantse Boerenlities in Contradanseu, c.1710

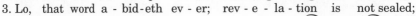

1. Light of a - ges and of na-tions, ev - ery race and ev - ery time
2. Rea-son's no - ble as - pi - ra - tion truth in grow-ing clear-ness saw;
3. Lo, that word a - bid-eth ev - er; rev - e - la - tion is not sealed;

has re - ceived thine in - spi-ra-tions, glimps-es of thy truth sub-lime.
con - science spoke its con-dem-na-tion, or pro-claimed e - ter - nal law.
an - swering now to our en - dea-vor, truth and right are still re-vealed.

al - ways spir-its in rapt vi-sion passed the heaven-ly veil with - in,
While thine in-ward rev - e - la-tions told thy saints their prayers were heard,
That which came to an-cient sag-es, Greek, Bar-bar - ian, Ro - man, Jew,

al - ways hearts bowed in con-tri-tion found sal - va-tion from their sin.
proph-ets to the guilt - y na-tions spoke thine ev - er - last - ing word.
writ-ten in the soul's deep pag-es, shines to - day, for - ev - er new.

If I Can Stop One Heart From Breaking

Emily Dickinson (1830–1886)
SMIT Irregular
Leo Smit (b. 1921)

If I can stop one heart from break-ing, I shall not live in vain. If I can ease one life the ach-ing or cool one pain, or help one faint - ing rob - in un - to his nest a - gain, I shall not live in vain.

The Human Touch Can Light the Flame

John Andrew Storey (b.1935)
DICKINSON COLLEGE L.M.
Lee Hastings Bristol, Jr. (1923–1979)

1. The hu-man touch can light the flame which gives a
bright-ness to the day, the spir-it us-es mor-tal
flame, life's ve-hi-cle for work and play.

2. The lov-er's kiss, the friend's em-brace, the clasp of
hands to show we care, the light of wel-come on the
face are treas-ured mo-ments all can share.

3. May all who come with-in our reach be kin-dled
by our in-ner glow, not just in spir-it's words we
preach, in hu-man touch love's faith we show.

Let Freedom Span Both East and West

Jacob Trapp (1899–1992)

McKEE C.M.

African-American Spiritual (c.1750–1875); adapt. & harm. Harry T. Burleigh (1866–1949)

1. Let free - dom span both east and west, and love both south and north, in u - ni - ver - sal fel - low - ship through - out the whole wide earth.

2. In beau - ty, won - der, ev - ery - where, let us com - mu - nion find; com - pas - sion be the gold - en cord close bind - ing hu - man - kind.

3. Be - yond all bar - ri - ers of race, of col - or, caste, or creed, let us make friend - ship, hu - man worth, our com - mon faith and deed.

4. Then east and west will meet and share, and south shall build with north, one hu - man com - mon - wealth of good through - out the whole wide earth.

Purest Blessing

Shaker; from Canterbury, NH

1. Shun the thorn and grow the flow - er,
   Speak no sen - ti - ment un - kind;
   Let thy life, like balm - y show - ers,
   Give sweet fra - grance to the mind.

2. Let thy deeds like sun - light fall - ing
   Where the shad - ows oft - en stray,
   And thy voice in lov - ing ac - cents
   Cheer the wea - ry o'er life's way!

3. Best, a - mid the pearls that glit - ter
   In the vic - tor's di - a - dem,
   Is the one of pur - est wa - ter—
   Love— the bril - liant, spark - ling gem.

For with days so swift - ly pass - ing,
We are all so prone to er - ror,
This the ha - lo of our Sav - iour,

Friends may go and come no more;
Gifts of love and gos - pel care
This the glo - ry of His strife,

Let them bear thy pur - est bless - ing,—
Are the sweet - est joys that min - gle
Let us weave its ra - diant bright - ness

Giv - ing but re - fills thy store.
With our bat - tle and our pray'r.
In the fab - ric of our life.

Now the Day Is Over

Sabine Baring-Gould (1834–1924); adapted
MERRIAL 6.5.6.5.
Joseph Barnby (1838–1936)

1. Now the day is o - ver, Night is draw - ing nigh,
2. Je - sus gave the wea - ry Calm and sweet re - pose,
3. Through the long night watch - es May thine an - gels spread
4. Glo - ry to the Fa - ther, Glo - ry to the Son,

Shad - ows of the eve - ning Steal a - cross the sky.
With thy ten - derest bless - ing May my eye - lids close.
Their white wings a - bove me Watch - ing round my bed.
And to Thee, blessed spir - it, While all a - ges run.

Immortal Love, Forever Full

John Greenleaf Whittier (1807–1892)
ST. COLUMBA 8.6.8.6.
Irish Melody; harm. Charles V. Stanford (1852–1924)

1. Im - mor - tal love, for - ev - er full, for - ev - er flow - ing free, for - ev - er shared, for - ev - er whole, a nev - er - end - ing sea!

2. Our out - ward lips con - fess the name all oth - er names a - bove; but love a - lone knows whence it came and com - pre - hen - deth love.

3. Blow, winds of love, a - wake and blow the mists of hate a - way; sing out, O Truth di - vine, and tell how wide and far we stray.

4. The let - ter fails, the sys - tems fall, and ev - ery sym - bol wanes; the Spir - it o - ver - see - ing all, E - ter - nal Love, re - mains.

PART 3

TRUTH THE POET SPEAKS

MANY WRITINGS tell us that the presence of God is always with His creation. And that God cherishes every thought and provides abundant opportunities for our souls to awaken to the wonders of His unlimited love. The truth, from which life has come to be and through which life endures, calls us to increasing awareness of the grand adventure of Creation. Agape love and a deepening awareness of humanity's relationship to life can encourage creativity and diversity.

Poetry may claim a special place in our world because it can sometimes push us beyond the simplifications we see every day. Through a woven tapestry of words, often the poet can help us recognize that diversities and constant changes show creativity in our universe. Poetry can speak of the grandeur of whirling galaxies and the mysteries of nature; help us become more aware of God's accelerating creation; express the innermost feelings of eternal love; and sing of noble deeds, mighty courage, and the majesty of humble service. The poet whispers to our longing souls, "There is more! There is more!"

Listen! Listen to the stirrings of truth the poet sings to your own loving soul. Listen to the spirit voice within that whispers of God's love. Listen to your Heart! It is in your Heart that you may learn many answers to life's questions. Listen to the glorious word-pictures painted by the poets of the holy energy that fills the world. Energy that is timeless, limitless, and invisible — energy that is God!

Your mind need not be confined to a narrow little channel. If you can listen closely, you may find an extraordinary change taking place within you, a change that comes without your asking, and in the change there can be great beauty and depth of reverent insight. Truths that the poet sings may help us become more aware that perhaps the visible and tangible are only tiny temporary manifestations of the underlying reality that could be called God.

The Elixir

Teach me, my God and King,
　In all things thee to see,
And what I do in anything,
　To do it as for thee:

Not rudely, as a beast,
　To run into an action;
But still to make thee prepossessed,
　And give it his perfection.

A man that looks on glass,
On it may stay his eye;
Or if he pleaseth, through it pass,
　And then the heaven espy.

All may of thee partake:
Nothing can be so mean,
Which with his tincture (for thy sake)
　Will not grow bright and clean.

A servant with this clause
　Makes drudgery divine:
Who sweeps a room, as for thy laws,
　Makes that and the action fine.

This is the famous stone
That turneth all to gold:
For that which God doth touch and own
　Cannot for less be told.

George Herbert

Every being in the universe
is an expression of the Tao.
It springs into existence,
unconscious, perfect, free,
takes on a physical body,
lets circumstances complete it.
That is why every being
spontaneously honors the Tao.

The Tao gives birth to all beings,
nourishes them, maintains them,
cares for them, comforts them, protects them,
takes them back to itself,
creating without possessing,
acting without expecting,
guiding without interfering.
That is why love of the Tao
is in the very nature of things.

Lao-Tzu. Translated by Stephen Mitchell.

The Builders

All are architects of Fate,
   Working in these walls of Time;
Some with massive deeds and great,
   Some with ornaments of rhyme.

Nothing useless is, or low;
   Each thing in its place is best;
And what seems but idle show
   Strengthens and supports the rest.

For the structure that we raise,
   Time is with materials filled;
Our to-days and yesterdays
   Are the blocks with which we build.

Truly shape and fashion these;
   Leave no yawning gaps between;
Think not, because no man sees,
   Such things will remain unseen.

In the elder days of Art,
   Builders wrought with greatest care
Each minute and unseen part;
   For the Gods see everywhere.

Let us do our work as well,
   Both the unseen and the seen!
Make the house, where God may dwell,
   Beautiful, entire, and clean.

Else our lives are incomplete,
   Standing in these walls of Time,

Broken stairways, where the feet
  Stumble as they seek to climb.

Build to-day, then, strong and sure,
  With a firm and ample base;
And ascending and secure
  Shall tomorrow find its place.

Thus alone can we attain
  To those turrets, where the eye
Sees the world as one vast plain,
  And one boundless reach of sky.

Henry Wadsworth Longfellow

Build thee more stately mansions, O my soul,
As the swift seasons roll!
Leave thy low-vaulted past!
Let each new temple, nobler than the last,
Shut thee from heaven with a dome more vast,
Til thou at length art free,
Leaving thine outgrown shell by life's unresting sea!

Oliver Wendell Holmes

This is an excerpt from Holmes's lengthy poem,
"The Chambered Nautilus."

The Head and the Heart

The head is stately, calm, and wise,
  And bears a princely part;
And down below in secret lies
  The warm, impulsive heart.

The lordly head that sits above,
  The heart that beats below,
Their several offices plainly prove,
  Their true relations show.

The head, erect, serene, and cool,
  Endowed with reason's art,
Was set aloft to guide and rule
  The throbbing, wayward heart.

And from the head, as from the higher,
  Comes every glorious thought;
And in the heart's transforming fire
  All noble deeds are wrought.

Yet each is best when both unite
  To make the man complete;
What were the heat without the light?
  The light without the heat?

  John Godfrey Saxe

Miracles

Why, who makes much of a miracle?
As to me, I know of nothing else but miracles,
Whether I walk the streets of Manhattan,
Or dart my sight over the roofs of houses toward the sky,
Or wade with naked feet along the beach just in the edge
    of the water,
Or stand under trees in the woods,
Or talk by day with any one I love,
Or sit at table at dinner with the rest,
Or look at strangers opposite me riding in the car,
Or watch honey-bees busy around the hive of a summer
    forenoon,
Or animals feeding in the fields,
Or the wonderfulness of the sundown, or of stars shining
    so quiet and bright,
Or the exquisite delicate thin curve of the new moon
    in spring;
These with the rest, one and all, are to me miracles,
The whole referring, yet each distinct and in its place.
To me every hour of the light and dark is a miracle,
Every cubic inch of space is a miracle,
Every square yard of the surface of the earth is spread
    with the same,
Every foot of the interior swarms with the same.

To me the sea is a continual miracle,
The fishes that swim—the rocks—the motion of the
    waves—the ships with men in them,
What stranger miracles are there?

    Walt Whitman

A Psalm of Life

*What the heart of the young man
said to the Psalmist*

Tell me not, in mournful numbers,
    Life is but an empty dream!—
For the soul is dead that slumbers,
    And things are not what they seem.

Life is real! Life is earnest!
    And the grave is not the goal;
Dust thou art, to dust returnest,
    Was not spoken of the soul.

Not enjoyment, and not sorrow,
    Is our destined end or way;
But to act, that each to-morrow
    Finds us farther than to-day.

Art is long, and Time is fleeting,
    And our hearts, though stout and brave,
Still, like muffled drums, are beating
    Funeral marches to the grave.

In the world's broad field of battle,
    In the bivouac of Life,
Be not like dumb, driven cattle!
    Be a hero in the strife!

Trust no Future, howe'er pleasant!
    Let the dead Past bury its dead!
Act,—act in the living Present!
    Heart within, and God o'erhead!

Lives of great men all remind us
    We can make our lives sublime,
And, departing, leave behind us
    Footprints on the sands of time.

Footprints, that perhaps another,
    Sailing o'er life's solemn main,
A forlorn and shipwrecked brother,
    Seeing, shall take heart again.

Let us, then, be up and doing,
    With a heart for any fate;
Still achieving, still pursuing,
    Learn to labor and to wait.

Henry Wadsworth Longfellow

Solitude

Laugh, and the world laughs with you;
Weep, and you weep alone,
For the sad old earth must borrow its mirth,
But has trouble enough of its own.
Sing, and the hills will answer;
Sigh, it is lost on the air,
The echoes bound to a joyful sound,
But shrink from voicing care.

Rejoice, and men will seek you;
Grieve, and they turn and go.
They want full measure of all your pleasure,
But they do not need your woe.
Be glad, and your friends are many;
Be sad, and you lose them all,—
There are none to decline your nectar'd wine,
But alone you must drink life's gall.

Feast, and your halls are crowded;
Fast, and the world goes by.
Succeed and give, and it helps you live,
But no man can help you die.
There is room in the halls of pleasure
For a large and lordly train,
But one by one we must all file on
Through the narrow aisles of pain.

Ella Wheeler Wilcox

Eternal Love

Spheres of light
in unbroken rhythm
wrap me around with new heaven.
My sense translucent,
and it is now
a softened, lulling eternity.

Inside
I am as sudden and whole
as a moment of lingering joy.
To radiate a word of this pearl
is to honor
the manner of loving.

  Janna Russell

Love is complete and sincere respect for another being. It is the
ecstasy of the true self. Love extends beyond all planes and is
limitless. After a million lives, and a million deaths it still lives.
And it only dwells in the heart and soul.

  Ken Wilber

What Is Love?

Love is the sun and the rain
    kissing the bud into bloom.
  Love is the flower
      giving its fragrant beauty
        to the air.
  Love is the dropping
    of the petals
    into the good soil
      to feed it
    with their joy.
Love is the openhearted receiving
  of the earth,
  and its giving again
    to the new seeds
  which fall therein.
Love is being what
    God created us to be.
  Love is being at peace
    with all humanity
      with all creation.
    Love is being one with God.

Verle Bell

What God Is Like

I did not know what God is like
Until a friendly word
Came to me in an hour of need—
And it was God I heard.

I did not know what God is like
Until I heard love's feet
On errands of God's mercy
Go up and down life's street.

I did not know what God is like
Until I felt a hand
Clasp mine and lift me when alone
I had no strength to stand.

I think I know what God is like,
For I have seen the face
Of God's son looking at me
From all the human race.

James Dillet Freeman

God Spoke to Me

Through the song of a bird
He announced His presence.
Through a golden sunrise
He shared some of His splendor.
Through a season of silence
He called me His child.
Through His word of Truth
He told me the Way.
Through the smile of a friend
He revealed His nature.
Through the eyes of an infant
He expressed His joy.
Through the sparkle of raindrops
He spoke of a miracle.
Through my time of indecision
He gave me the answer.

William Arthur Ward

Be at peace with your own soul, then heaven and earth will be at peace with you. Enter eagerly into the treasure house that is within you, you will see the things that are in heaven; for there is but one single entry to them both. The ladder that leads to the Kingdom is hidden within your soul. . . . Dive into yourself, and in your soul you will discover the stairs by which to ascend.

Saint Isaac of Nineveh

My Love to Thee

The hours I've spent with Thee, dear Lord,
   Are pearls of priceless worth to me.
My soul, my being merge in sweet accord,
   In love for Thee, in love for Thee.

Each hour a pearl, each pearl a prayer,
   Binding Thy presence close to me;
I only know that Thou art there,
   And I am lost in Thee.

Oh, glorious joys that thrill and bless!
   Oh, visions sweet of love divine!
My soul with rapturous bliss can ill express
   That Thou art mine, O Lord! that Thou art mine!

Myrtle Fillmore. Adapted from "The Rosary."

Intimations of Immortality

There was a time when meadow, grove, and stream
   The earth, and every common sight,
To me did seem
   Apparell'd in celestial light,
The glory and the freshness of a dream.
It is not now as it hath been of yore;—
     Turn whereso'er I may,
      By night or day,
The things which I have seen I now can see no more.
     The rainbow comes and goes,
     And lovely is the rose;
     The moon doth with delight
   Look round her when the heavens are bars;
     Waters on a starry night
     Are beautiful and fair;
   The sunshine is a glorious birth;
   But yet I know, where'er I go,
That there has pass'd away a glory from the earth.

Our birth is but a sleep and a forgetting:
The Soul that rises with us, our life's Star,
    Hath had elsewhere its setting,
     And cometh from afar:
    Not in entire forgetfulness,
    And not in utter nakedness,
But trailing clouds of glory do we come
    From God, who is our home:
Heaven lies about us in our infancy!
Shades of the prison-house begin to close
    Upon the growing boy,

But he beholds the light, and whence it flows,
     He sees it in his joy;
The Youth, who daily farther from the east
  Must travel, still is Nature's priest,
    And by the vision splendid
    Is on his way attended;

At length the Man perceives it die away,
And fade into the light of common day.

    O joy! that in our embers
    Is something that doth live,
    That nature yet remembers
    What was so fugitive!

William Wordsworth, from The Ode

Hold on to what is good
   even if it is a handful of earth.
Hold on to what you believe
   even if it is a tree which stands by itself.
Hold on to what you must do
   even if it is a long way from here.
Hold on to life
   even when it is easier letting go.
Hold on to my hand
   even when I have gone away from you.

Pueblo (North America)

God Is in the Midst of Me

Where is God? Is He afar,
Out beyond the farthest star?
No, He is not far but near;
He is nearer than my fear,
He is nearer than my need.
When I call Him He will heed;
He is in the midst of me!

When the way uncertain is,
He will hold my hand in His;
In the valley of the night
I will have an inward light.
He is faith—I will not fear;
He is love, and He will hear;
He is in the midst of me.

Need I even call at all?
Knows He not each sparrow's fall?
Lord Immanuel, Thou art
Ever present in my heart,
And however far I roam
In Thy heart I am at home;
Thou art in the midst of me!

James Dillet Freeman

Song of the Open Road

Afoot and light-hearted, I take to the open road,
healthy, free, the world before me.
   Henceforth I ask not good fortune—
   I myself am good-fortune;
   Strong and content,
   I travel the open road.
I inhale great draughts of space;
the east and the west are mine,
and the north and the south are mine.
   All seems beautiful to me;
   I can repeat over to men and women,
   You have done such good to me,
   I would do the same to you.
Wherever you are, come travel with me!
However sweet these laid-up stores—however convenient
     this dwelling, we cannot remain here;
  However sheltered this port, and however calm these
     waters, we must not anchor here.
Together! the inducements shall be greater;
We will sail pathless and wild seas;
  We will go where winds blow, waves dash, and the Yankee
     clipper speeds by under full sail.
Forward! after the great Companions!
and to belong to them!
They, too, are on the road!
  Onward! to that which is endless,
  as it was beginningless,
  To undergo much, tramps of days, rests of nights.
To see nothing anywhere but what you may reach it
     and pass it.

To look up or down no road but it stretches and waits
for you—
To know the universe itself as a road—
as many roads—
as roads for traveling souls.

Walt Whitman

God Give Me Joy

God give me joy in the common things:
In the dawn that lures, the eve that sings.

In the new grass sparkling after rain,
In the late wind's wild and weird refrain;

In the springtime's spacious field of gold,
In the precious light by winter doled.

God give me joy in the love of friends,
In their dear home talks as summer ends;

In the songs of children, unrestrained;
In the sober wisdom age has gained.

God give me joy in the tasks that press,
In the memories that burn and bless;

In the thought that life has love to spend,
In the faith that God's at journey's end.

God give me hope for each day that springs,
God give me joy in the common things!

Thomas Curtis Clark

The Vision

I stood quietly in a fragrant meadow and looked toward
    a high and majestic mountain.
There, on the mountainside, I beheld men and women
    and children
from all nations of the earth, from many cultures, and
    of many spiritual beliefs.
They were standing with their hands joined in fellowship.
Each one looked directly into the eyes of the others,
    and no one was afraid.
A soft radiance of love seemed to fill the air with shimmering
    loveliness.
The essence of peace permeated the air with majesty
    and grace.
I asked the Angel by my side, "Pray tell, what place is this?"
The Angel smiled at me and replied, "This is Heaven."

Heaven? I thought Heaven was a place of perfect harmony
    and all-powerful love;
a place of the celebration of life eternal. "It is!" the Angel
    responded.
I thought for a moment, then asked the Angel, "Pray tell,
    where is this place?"
The Angel answered, "In the consciousness of your
    precious heart."
Again, I pondered the situation, observing the serenity
    and love all around me.
I asked the Angel, "*When* does this happen?"
And the Angel said, "When all people, throughout all the earth
learn to love one another as God has ever loved you!"

    Rebecca Clark

It Couldn't Be Done

Somebody said that it couldn't be done,
　　But he with a chuckle replied,
That "maybe it couldn't," but he would be one
　　Who wouldn't say so till he'd tried.
So he buckled right in with the trace of a grin
　　On his face. If he worried, he hid it.
He started to sing as he tackled the thing
　　That couldn't be done, and he did it.

Somebody scoffed: "Oh, you'll never do that;
　　At least no one ever has done it;"
But he took off his coat and he took off his hat,
　　And the first thing we knew he'd begun it.
With a lift of his chin and a bit of a grin,
　　Without any doubting or quiddit,
He started to sing as he tackled the thing
　　That couldn't be done, and he did it.

There are thousands to tell you it cannot be done,
　　There are thousands to prophesy failure;
There are thousands to point out to you, one by one,
　　The dangers that wait to assail you.
But just buckle in with a bit of a grin,
　　Just take off your coat and go do it;
Just start to sing as you tackle the thing
　　That "cannot be done," and you'll do it.

Edgar A. Guest

I Am There

Do you need Me?
I am there.
You cannot see Me, yet I am the light you see by.
You cannot hear Me, yet I speak through your voice.
You cannot feel Me, yet I am the power at work in your hands.
I am at work, though you do not understand My ways.
I am at work, though you do not recognize My works.
I am not strange visions. I am not mysteries.
Only in absolute stillness, beyond self, can you know Me
   as I am, and
then but as a feeling and a faith.
Yet I am there. Yet I hear. Yet I answer.
When you need Me, I am there.
Even if you deny Me, I am there.
Even when you feel most alone, I am there.
Even in your fears, I am there.
Even in your pain, I am there.
I am there when you pray and when you do not pray.
I am in you, and you are in Me.
Only in your mind can you feel separate from Me, for only
   in your mind
are the mists of "yours" and "mine."
Yet only in your mind can you know Me and experience Me.
Empty your heart of empty fears.
When you get yourself out of the way, I am there.
You can of yourself do nothing, but I can do all.
And I am in all.
Though you may not see the good, good is there, for I am there.
I am there because I have to be, because I am.
Only in Me does the world have meaning; only out of Me
   does the
world take form; only because of Me does the world go forward.

I am the law on which the movement of the stars
    and the growth of
living cells are founded.
I am the love that is the law's fulfilling.
I am assurance.
I am peace.
I am oneness.
I am the law that you can live by.
I am the love that you can cling to.
I am your assurance.
I am your peace.
I am one with you.
I am..
 Though you fail to find Me, I do not fail you.
Though your faith in Me is unsure, My faith in you never
    wavers,
because I know you, because I love you.
Beloved, I am there.

James Dillet Freeman

At the end of life, our questions are very simple:
Did I live fully? Did I love well?

Jack Kornfield

Love

On all that the Lord laboured He lavished His love.
Love is the plant of peace, most precious of virtues;
All heaven could not hold it, so heavy in itself,
It fell in fulness forth on the field of earth
And of the folds of that field took flesh and blood;
No leaf thereafter on a linden tree was ever lighter,
No needle-point so piercing or nimble to handle,
No armour can withhold it or high walls hinder.
Therefore is Love leader of the Lord's folk in heaven,
And, to know its nature, it is nurtured in power,
And in the heart is its home and fountain-head.
Instinctively at heart a strength is stirring
Flowing to the Father that formed us all,
Looked on us with love, and let His Son die,
Meekly, for our misdoings, to amend us all.
Yet appointed He no punishment for the pain they put
    Him to,
But meekly with His mouth besought mercy for them,
And pity for the people that were putting Him to death.
See it an example, only seen in Him,
That He was mighty and yet meek, and had mercy to grant
To those that hung Him on high and thrust Him through
    the heart.
So I recommend you rich ones to have pity on the poor,
To comfort the care-stricken, the sin-encumbered.
Love, the most pleasant thing that our Lord pleads for us,
Is also the ready roadway, running into heaven.

   William Langland

As once the wingèd energy of delight
carried you over childhood's dark abysses,
now beyond your own life build the great
arch of unimagined bridges.

Wonders happen if we can succeed
in passing through the harshest danger;
but only in a bright and purely granted
achievement can we realize the wonder.

To work *with* Things in the indescribable
relationship is not too hard for us;
the pattern grown more intricate and subtle,
and being swept along is not enough.

Take your practiced powers and stretch them out
until they span the chasm between two
contradictions . . . For the god
wants to know himself in you.

    Rainer Maria Rilke. Translated by Stephen Mitchell.

Pass It On

Have you had a kindness shown?
　　Pass it on.
'Twas not given for thee alone,
　　Pass it on.
Let it travel down the years,
Let it wipe another's tears,
'Till in heav'n the deed appears—
　　Pass it on.

Did you hear the loving word?
　　Pass it on.
Like the singing of a bird?
　　Pass it on.
Let its music live and grow
Let it cheer another's woe;
You have reaped what others sow—
　　Pass it on.

'Twas the sunshine of a smile—
　　Pass it on.
Staying but a little while!
　　Pass it on.
April beam a little thing,
Still it wakes the flowers of spring,
Makes the silent birds to sing—
　　Pass it on.

　　Henry Burton

My Spirit Longeth for Thee

My spirit longeth for Thee,
  Within my troubled breast
Altho' I be unworthy
  Of so divine a Guest.

Of so divine a Guest,
  Unworthy tho' I be,
Yet has my heart no rest,
  Unless it come from Thee.

Unless it come from Thee,
  In vain I look around;
In all that I can see,
  No rest is to be found.

No rest is to be found,
  But in Thy blessed love;
O! let my wish be crown'd,
  And send it from above!

John Byrom

What Lies Beyond?

Beyond the farthest cape, what lies?
Beyond the islands of surmise,
The shallow waters where we ply
Our lives, beyond the reach of eye
Or even thought, what lies out there?
Sometimes I stand for hours and stare
Out, out beyond imagining.
The waves that break around me bring
Only a sense of more, yet more.
I think there is no farthest shore.
O God, where shall the limits be?
Your pattern is infinity.

James Dillet Freeman

Before me peaceful
Behind me peaceful
Under me peaceful
Over me peaceful
Around me peaceful

Navajo (North America)

All things in this creation exist within you, and all things in you exist in creation; there is no border between you and the closest things, and there is no distance between you and the farthest things, and all things, from the lowest to the loftiest, from the smallest to the greatest, are within you as equal things. In one atom are found all the elements of the earth; In one motion of the mind are found the motions of all the laws of existence; in one drop of water are found the secrets of all the endless oceans; in one aspect of *you* are found all the aspects of *existence* . . . [Thus] "Your life has no end, and you shall live forevermore."

Kahlil Gibran

Glass House Canticle

Bless Thee, O Lord, for the living arc of the sky over me
this morning.

Bless Thee, O Lord, for the companionship of the night mist
far above the skyscraper peaks I saw when I woke once during
the night.

Bless Thee, O Lord, for the miracle of light to my eyes and
the mystery of it ever changing.

Bless Thee, O Lord, for the laws Thou hast ordained holding
fast these tall oblongs of stone and steel, holding fast the plan-
et Earth in its course and farther beyond the cycle of the Sun.

   Carl Sandburg

The Road Not Taken

Two roads diverged in a yellow wood,
And sorry I could not travel both
And be one traveler, long I stood
And looked down one as far as I could
To where it bent in the undergrowth;

Then took the other, as just as fair,
And having perhaps the better claim,
Because it was grassy and wanted wear;
Though as for that the passing there
Had worn them really about the same,

And both that morning equally lay
In leaves no step had trodden black.
Oh, I kept the first for another day!
Yet knowing how way leads on to way,
I doubted if I should ever come back.

I shall be telling this with a sigh
Somewhere ages and ages hence:
Two roads diverged in a wood, and I—
I took the one less traveled by,
And that has made all the difference.

Robert Frost

Bond and Free

Love has earth to which she clings
With hills and circling arms about—
Wall within wall to shut fear out.
But Thought has need of no such things,
For Thought has a pair of dauntless wings.

On snow and sand and turf, I see
Where Love has left a printed trace
With straining in the world's embrace.
And such is Love and glad to be.
But Thought has shaken his ankles free.

Thought cleaves the interstellar gloom
And sits in Sirius' disc all night,
Till day makes him retrace his flight,
With smell of burning on every plume,
Back past the sun to an earthly room.

His gains in heaven are what they are.
Yet some say Love by being thrall
And simply staying possesses all
In several beauty that Thought fares far
To find fused in another star.

Robert Frost

Our Hold on the Planet

We asked for rain. It didn't flash and roar.
It didn't lose its temper at our demand
And blow a gale. It didn't misunderstand
And give us more than our spokesman bargained for;
And just because we owned to a wish for rain,
Send us a flood and bid us be damned and drown.
It gently threw us a glittering shower down.
And when we had taken that into the roots of grain,
It threw us another and then another still
Till the spongy soil again was natal wet.
We may doubt the just proportion of good to ill.
There is much in nature against us. But we forget:
Take nature altogether since time began,
Including human nature, in peace and war,
And it must be a little more in favor of man,
Say a fraction of one per cent at the very least,
Or our number living wouldn't be steadily more,
Our hold on the planet wouldn't have so increased.

Robert Frost

'Tis Love that Moveth the Celestial Spheres

'Tis love that moveth the celestial spheres
In endless yearning for the Changeless One,
And the stars sing together, as they run
To number the innumerable years.
'Tis love that lifteth through their dewy tears
The roses' beauty to the heedless sun,
And with no hope, nor any guerdon won,
Love leads me on, nor end of love appears.
For the same breath that did awake the flowers,
Making them happy with a joy unknown,
Kindled my light and fixed my spirit's goal;
And the same hand that reined the flying hours
And chained the whirling earth to Phoebus's throne,
In love's eternal orbit keeps the soul.

   George Santayana

To see a World in a Grain of Sand
and a Heaven in a Wild Flower,
hold Infinity in the palm of your hand
and Eternity in an hour.

   William Blake

There is a love like a small lamp, which goes out when the oil is consumed; or like a stream, which dries up when it doesn't rain. But there is a love that is like a mighty spring gushing up out of the earth; it keeps flowing forever, and is inexhaustible.

Saint Isaac of Nineveh

When you look at the world in a narrow way, how narrow
  it seems!
When you look at it in a mean way, how mean it is!
When you look at it selfishly, how selfish it is!
But when you look at it as a broad, generous, friendly spirit,
What wonderful people you find in it!

Horace Rutledge

Precious Seed

In what we live, in what we read,
In what we share with another's need,
In how we grow, to what aspire,
In lifting our vision ever higher;
In deeds of kindness and words of praise,
In quiet hours and busy days,
In little things that are great indeed,
We sow the kingdom's precious seed.

    Russell A. Kemp

The more love we give away, the more we have left.
The laws of love differ from the laws of arithmetic.
Love hoarded dwindles, but love given grows. If we
give all our love, we will have more left than he who
saves some. Giving love, not receiving, is important;
but when we give without thought of receiving, we
automatically and inescapably receive abundantly.
Heaven is a by-product of love. When we say, "I love
you," we mean that "a little of God's love flows from
me to you." Thereby, we do not love less, but more.
For in flowing, the quantity is magnified.

    John Marks Templeton

Student, do the simple purification.
You know that the seed is inside the horse-chestnut tree;
and inside the seed there are the blossoms of the tree,
    and the chestnuts, and the shade.
So inside the human body there is the seed, and inside
    the seed there is the human body again.

Fire, air, earth, water, and space—if you don't want
    the secret one,
You can't have these either.

Thinkers, listen, tell me what you know of that is not
    inside the soul?
Take a pitcher full of water and set it down on the water—
now it has water inside and water outside.
We mustn't give it a name,
lest silly people start talking again about the body
    and the soul.

If you want the truth, I'll tell you the truth:
Listen to the secret sound, the real sound, which is inside you.
The one no one talks of speaks the secret sound to himself,
and he is the one who has made it all.

   Kabir. Translated by Robert Bly.

Possibilities

Where are the poets, unto whom belong
    the Olympian heights; whose singing shafts were sent
    straight to the mark, and not from bows half bent,
    but with the utmost tension of the thong?
Where are the stately argosies of song,
    whose rushing keels made music as they went
    sailing in search of some new continent,
    with all sail set, and steady winds and strong?
Perhaps there lives some dreamy boy, untaught
    in schools, some graduate of the field or street,
    who shall become a master of the art,
An admiral sailing the high seas of thought,
    fearless and first, and steering with his fleet
    for lands not yet laid down in any chart.

    Henry Wadsworth Longfellow

Hope Is the Thing with Feathers

Hope is the thing with feathers
That perches in the soul
And sings the tune without the words
And never stops at all.

And sweetest in the gale is heard;
And sore must be the storm
That could abash the little bird
That kept so many warm.

I've heard it in the chillest land
And on the strangest sea,
Yet never in extremity
It asked a crumb of me.

Emily Dickinson

Antiphon for the Holy Spirit

Holy Spirit,
giving life to all life,
moving all creatures,
root of all things,
washing them clean,
wiping out their mistakes,
healing their wounds,
you are our true life,
luminous, wonderful,
awakening the heart
from its ancient sleep.

Hildegard of Bingen

Gandhi once said, "What I am concerned with is my readiness
to obey the call of Truth, my God, from moment to moment,
no matter how inconsistent it may appear. My commitment is
to Truth, not to consistency." May we, like Gandhi, see our lives
as a series of experiments with the truth and make every effort
to align our choices with the deeper truths of the universe.

from spiralling ecstatically this

proud nowhere of earth's most prodigious night
blossoms a newborn babe:around him,eyes
—gifted with every keener appetite
than mere unmiracle can quite appease—
humbly in their imagined bodies kneel
(over time space doom dream while floats the whole

perhapsless mystery of paradise)

mind without soul may blast some universe
to might have been,and stop ten thousand stars
but not one heartbeat of this child;nor shall
even prevail a million questionings
against the silence of his mother's smile

—whose only secret all creation sings

E.E.Cummings

When the mind is at peace,
the world too is at peace.
Nothing real, nothing absent.
Not holding on to reality,
not getting stuck in the void,
you are neither holy nor wise, just
an ordinary fellow who has completed his work.

   Layman P'ang

If you look for truth outside yourself,
it gets farther and farther away.
Today, walking alone,
I meet him everywhere I step.
He is the same as me,
yet I am not him.
Only if you understand it in this way
will you merge with the way things are.

   Tung-Shan Liang-Chieh

Each member of the human race, at the outset of his or her individual life story, is one sole cell vibrating with the radiant life of God. As these cells multiply, they become a society that is familial and a unity—an organized family of cells, with corporate individuality.

When we come to birth, a wondrous universe awaits us, filled with all its splendid and awe-inspiring aspects, its beauty and its bounty. As the unhurried stars wheel above a thousand million hearts, could Love be like the tree which shows the first signs of growth when the shoot blossoms, and provide the sheltering bower of oneness and harmony where all may worship God in Truth and Light.

Rebekah Alezander

Leave this chanting and singing and telling of beads! Whom dost thou worship in this lonely dark corner of a temple with doors all shut? Open thine eyes and see, thy God is not before thee.

He is there where the tiller is tilling the hard ground and the pathmaker is breaking stones. He is with them in sun and in shower, and his garment is covered with dust.

Put off thy holy mantle and even like him come down on the dusty soil!

Deliverance? Where is this deliverance to be found? Our master himself has joyfully taken upon him the bonds of creation; he is bound with us all for ever.

Rabindranath Tagore

Where Thou Art, There Is Heaven

My Lord God, my All in All, Life of my life, Spirit of my spirit, look in mercy upon me and so fill me with Your Holy Spirit that my heart shall have no room for love of aught but You. I seek from You no other gift but Yourself who are the giver of life and all its blessings. From You I ask not for the world or its treasures, nor yet for heaven even make request, but You alone do I desire and long for, and where You are, there is heaven. The hunger and the thirst of this heart of mine can be satisfied only with You who have given me birth. O my Creator! You have created my heart for Yourself alone, and not for another. Therefore this heart can find no rest or ease save in You, in You who have both created it and set in it this very longing for rest. Take away then from my heart all that is opposed to You, and enter and abide and rule forever.

Sadhu Sundar Singh

We never know how high we are
Till we are called to rise
And then, if we are true to plan
Our statures touch the skies—

The Heroism we recite
Would be a normal thing
Did not ourselves the Cubits warp
For fear to be a King—

Emily Dickinson

That Love is all there is,
Is all we know of Love;
It is enough, the freight should be
Proportioned to the groove.

Emily Dickinson

The fruit of silence is prayer,
The fruit of prayer is faith,
The fruit of faith is love and
The fruit of love is silence.

Mother Teresa

The Quiet Mind

Empty your mind of all thoughts.
Let your heart be at peace.
Watch the turmoil of beings,
but contemplate their return.

Each separate being in the universe
returns to the common source.
Returning to the source is serenity.

If you don't realize the source,
you stumble in confusion and sorrow.
When you realize where you come from,
you naturally become tolerant,
disinterested, amused,
kind-hearted as a grandmother,
dignified as a king.
Immersed in the wonder of the Tao,
you can deal with whatever life brings you,
and when death comes, you are ready.

Lao-Tzu. Translated by Stephen Mitchell.

Where There's a Will, There's a Way

"Aut viam inveniam, aut faciam."

It was a noble Roman,
   In Rome's imperial day,
Who heard a coward croaker,
   Before the Castle, say:
"They're safe in such a fortress;
   There is no way to shake it!"
"On—on!" exclaimed the hero,
   "I'll find a way, or make it!"

Is *Fame* your aspiration?
   Her path is steep and high;
In vain he seeks her temple,
   Content to gaze and sign;
The shining throne is waiting,
   But he alone can take it
Who says, with Roman firmness
   "I'll find a way, or make it!"

Is *Learning* your ambition?
   There is no royal road;
Alike the peer and peasant
   Must climb to her abode:
Who feels the thirst of knowledge
   In Helicon may slake it,
If he has still the Roman will
   "To find a way, or make it!"

Are *Riches* worth the getting?
    They must be bravely sought;
With wishing and with fretting
    The boom cannot be bought:

To all the prize is open,
But only he can take it
Who says, with Roman courage,
"*I'll find a way, or make it!*"

In *Love's* impassioned warfare
    The tale has ever been
That victory crowns the valiant,—
    The brave are they who win:
Though strong is Beauty's castle,
    A lover still may take it,
Who says with Roman daring,
    "*I'll find a way, or make it!*"

    John Godfrey Saxe

Pandora Song

I stood within the heart of God;
It seemed a place that I had known:
(I was blood-sister to the clod,
Blood-brother to the stone.)

I found my love and labor there,
My house, my raiment, meat and wine,
My ancient rage, my old despair,—
Yea, all things that were mine.

I saw the spring and summer pass,
The trees grow bare, and winter come;
All was the same as once it was
Upon my hills at home.

Then suddenly in my own heart
I felt God walk and gaze about;
He spoke: his words seemed held apart
With gladness and with doubt.

"Here is my meat and wine," He said,
"My love, my toil, my ancient care;
Here is my cloak, my book, my bed,
And here my old despair.

"Here are my seasons: winter, spring,
Summer the same, and autumn spills
The fruits I look for; everything
As on my heavenly hills."

William Vaughn Moody

The Dawn

One morn I rose and looked upon the world.
"Have I been blind until this hour?" I said.
On every trembling leaf the sun had spread,
And was like a golden tapestry unfurled;
And as the moments passed more light was hurled
Upon the drinking earth athirst for light;
And I, beholding all this wondrous sight,
Cried out aloud, "O God, I love Thy world!"
And since that waking, often I drink deep
The joy of dawn, and peace abides with me;
And although I know that I again shall see
Dark fear with withered hand approach my sleep,
More sure am I when lonely night shall flee,
At dawn the sun will bring good cheer to me.

Author unknown

Effortlessly,
Love flows from God into man,
Like a bird
Who rivers the air
Without moving her wings.
Thus we move in His world
One in body and soul,
 Though outwardly separate in form.
As the Source strikes the note,
Humanity sings—
The Holy Spirit is our harpist,
And all strings
Which are touched in Love
Must sound.

Mechtild of Magdeburg. Translated by Jane Hirshfield.

If we are to achieve a richer culture, rich in contrasting values, we must recognize the whole gamut of human potentialities, and so weave a less arbitrary social fabric, one in which each diverse human gift will find a resting place.

Margaret Mead

The Secret

I met God in the morning
  When my day was at its best,
And His presence came like sunrise,
  Like a glory in my breast.

All day long the Presence lingered,
  All day long He stayed with me,
And we sailed in perfect calmness
  O'er a very troubled sea.

Other ships were blown and battered,
  Other ships were sore distressed,
But the winds that seemed to drive them
  Brought to us a peace and rest.

Then I thought of other mornings,
  With a keen remorse of mind,
When I too had loosed the moorings,
  With the Presence left behind.

So I think I know the secret,
  Learned from many a troubled way;
You must seek Him in the morning
  If you want Him through the day!

  Ralph Spaulding Cushman

The Larger Prayer

At first I prayed for Light:
  Could I but see the way,
How gladly, swiftly would I walk
  To everlasting day!

And next I prayed for Strength:
  That I might tread the road
With firm, unfaltering feet, and win
  The heaven's serene abode.

And then I asked for Faith:
  Could I but trust my God,
I'd live enfolded in His peace,
  Though foes were all abroad.

But now I pray for Love:
  Deep love to God and man,
A living love that will not fail,
  However dark His plan.

And Light and Strength and Faith
  Are opening everywhere;
God only waited for me, till
  I prayed the larger prayer.

Ednah D. Cheney

Affirmation of a Seeking Heart

The Living Light of God is the Truth of my soul.
The Presence of God's Love guides
    every sure step of my journey of life.
Yes! Creator God,—the presence of Light, Peace,
Joy, Love, Life and Humility—is ever
    within, about, before, and beside me.

I am a child of God.
In God's Love and Light I live and move and have my being.
Where there is Light, there can be no darkness.
I daily look to the Light of Truth and bring
    Its sweet radiance into the prism of my soul.
I hold the thought that whatever I do this day and every day,
    I do in God's loving Light.
Although clouds may appear on the horizon of my world,
Never for one moment does the promise
    Of God's Presence grow dim or fade.
It shines freely, clearly, steadily, and brightly,
    Permanently!
I acknowledge the Light of God in my life.
I choose to live in the Light.
I work in the Light.
I play in the Light.
I am lovingly enfolded in the Light.
The living, loving Light of God is with me always.
I am grateful and joyfully give thanks for the Light.
    I go forth now to do all that needs to be done by me.
    And the Light that is true for me,
    Is true for all of God's children!
    And so it is!

Rebecca Clark

Within the Depths of Me

The heights I reach, the worlds I touch,
    The wonders that I dream of,
Or all the things I ever wished
    Or ever could conceive of
Are things beyond, and things below,
    And things that cannot be,
Except for those that live and grow
    Within the depths of me.
So very deep and hidden that,
    Save for times like these,
I can only dream of them
    And wish that they could be
A thing apart, a thing alive,
    A thing that I could see,
A thing to touch, a thing to hold,
    A thing to comfort me.
But if I watch, and if I wait,
    And hold to all that's true,
There will come a time, and then a place,
    And what I'll see is You.
For You are what I dream of,
    The things that cannot be,
Except for those that live and grow
    Within the depths of me.

    Kalar Walters

Birth—Awareness!

The whisper of wings—
The crisp feel of straw beneath
   my soft new body—
Do I hear the tinkle of little bells
That encircle the neck of that beast,
   and the bleating of a little lamb?
What adoration in the beautiful
   countenance gazing down at me,
While the arm encased in coarse
   linen embraces me yet so tenderly!
Is that the glitter of princely raiment
   rustling in the shadows?
 Do I smell the fragrance of incense and
   spices—pungent and so familiar?
In awe and wonder I catch glimpses
Of a dark blue canopy far above me
   studded with a host of twinkling lights!
And the taste of fresh night air as it brushes
   my lips and caresses my cheek so softly.
The question forms, and lingers, hovering
   over the precious tableau—
Will I fill the world with love?
It is all so right and perfect—
   I am here.

   Laurie Killam

The Answer

When for a purpose
I had prayed and prayed and prayed
Until my words seemed worn and bare
    With arduous use,
And I had knocked and asked and
    knocked and asked again,
And all my fervor and persistence brought no hope,
I paused to give my weary brain a rest
And ceased my anxious human cry.
    In that still moment,
After self had tried and failed,
There came a glorious vision of God's power,
And, lo, my prayer was answered in that hour.

Lowell Fillmore

The Light shines and lives in all. May I never forget that the darkest of creatures is also of the Light . . .

Love breeds love and is born and nurtured from tolerance and acceptance. Let me lay down the anxieties and frustrations in this life to seek and foster love all the while remaining unattached to the act and its results. . .

Spirit, friend of my flight, help me to journey homeward in view of your message, "Love binds all wounds, softens all roads, and frees the soul to fly home in peace."

Diane V. Cirincione

Courtesy

Of courtesy it is much less
Than courage of heart or holiness,
Yet in my walks it seems to me
That the Grace of God is in courtesy.

On monks I did in Storrington fall,
They took me straight into their hall;
I saw three pictures on a wall
And courtesy was in them all.

The first the Annunciation;
The second the Visitation,
The third the Consolation,
Of God that was Our Lady's Son.

The first was of Saint Gabriel;
On wings of flame from heaven he fell;
And as he went upon one knee
He shone with heavenly courtesy.

Our Lady out of Nazareth rode—
It was her month of heavy load;
Yet was her face both great and kind,
For Courtesy was in her mind.

The third, it was our little Lord,
Whom all the Kings in arms adored;
He was so small you could not see
His large intent of Courtesy.

Our Lord, that was our Lady's Son,
Go bless you, People, one by one;
My Rhyme is written, my work is done.

Hilaire Belloc

PART 4

LET EVERY HEART
WORSHIP OUR CREATOR

HAVE YOU EVER THOUGHT of the spoken word as being like a seedling, perhaps newly sprung from the heart of its creator? A word may seem like a simple thing in the originator's mind and yet—even in the embyronic stage—it brings form to an idea and prepares to launch that idea into expression. Fill words with thought and wing them with sincerity and faith and something powerful and potent may be born! Thus, it would seem to be most important that our words be words of truth, eternal words. These words can express the truth about God and God's relationship to His creation. Words can provide avenues for expression of worship in a multitude of ways—prayers, poems, hymns, prose! Words can reveal the true nature of humanity, our relationship to our Creator, to the universe, and to our fellow man.

When our words are offered to another in friendship, they can be like a healing balm that binds the wound that sorrow feels. They can lift the pall of loneliness and enfold a tender heart with loving, compassionate energy. And when we go apart to pray in quietness and confidence that God will hear and heed our prayer, the powerful energy of our words can be as thrilling as the morning's choir of birdsong outside our window.

How fulfilling can be the day that is begun with an idea, a word, or a prayer that is positive, uplifting, and inspiring. Often in life we may find that people respond to us in the manner in which we inspire them to act because of our attitude, our disposition, and our words! Let's keep our ears open to the words we speak. Listen to them carefully. In fact, if for one day we had to listen to every word that we spoke—really *listen*—we would surely attempt to govern our thoughts before we voiced them!

God within us knows the sincerity of our hearts and our true desire, and divine wisdom often provides the words to convey our ideas to others in ways that can be uplifting. The words of great teachers along the way—Jesus, Buddha, Confucius, Lao Tzu, Muhammed, and others—have inspired listeners and readers to leave a particular way of life and live a better, more fruitful life. Some of the words shared in this section of our book have served as that guiding light for travelers along the way. As you read the following pieces we have gathered, listen. Listen! And listen!

Listen!

Listen—and when you speak a word—
Think—is it worthy to be heard?
And will it bring uplifting cheer
When it meets the hearer's ear?

Perhaps it's better left unsaid,
Discarded, as a hueless thread
Lest pattern set within the loom
Be shot with anger, doubt, or gloom.

Is it helpful? And is it true?
Arising from the best in you?
Let us put all our words to test
In order that they be as blest,

As those of Christ who, faced with strife,
Spoke words of spirit, truth, and life.
Lord, gracious speech we would proclaim,
In faith, love, truth, and in Thy name!

Harold Whaley

The Basic Principle of All Religions

The great truth we are considering is the fundamental principle running through all religions. We find it in each one. In regard to it all agree. It is, moreover, a great truth in regard to which all people can agree, whether they belong to the same or to different religions. People always quarrel about the trifles, about their personal views of minor insignificant points. They always come together in the presence of great fundamental truths, the threads of which run through all. The quarrels are in connection with the lower self, the agreements are in connection with the higher self....

This mighty truth which we have agreed on as the great central fact of human life is the golden thread that runs through all religions. When we make it the paramount fact in our lives we will find that minor differences, narrow prejudices, and all these laughable absurdities will so fall away by virtue of their insignificance that a Jew can worship equally as well in a Catholic cathedral, a Catholic in a Jewish synagogue, a Buddhist in a Christian church, a Christian in a Buddhist temple. Or all can worship equally well about their own hearthstones or out on the hillside or while pursuing the avocations of everyday life. For true worship only God and the human soul are necessary. It does not depend on times or seasons or occasions. Anywhere and at any time God and man in the bush may meet.

Ralph Waldo Trine

Judaism

Among the world's major extant of historical religions, Judaism may well be the oldest. If we date its origin to the Exodus from Egypt some 3,200 years ago, only certain aspects of Hinduism can claim equal antiquity. Judaism can be viewed as the evolution of a people in the grip of two towering great ideas. The first is the idea of One God—imageless, primordially creative, and utterly transcendent—who, nevertheless cares for the creation. The second is the idea of human dignity: men and women become fully human only by responding to the moral intuitions divinely etched in their hearts. Judaism is the parent tradition from which both Christianity and Islam sprang.

The Ten Commandments: Exodus 20:2–17

1. I am the Lord your God, who brought you out of the land of Egypt, out of the house of bondage. You shall have no other gods before me.

2. You shall not make for yourself a graven image, or any likeness of anything that is in heaven above, or that is in the earth beneath, or that is in the water under the earth; you shall not bow down to them or serve them....

3. You shall not take the name of the Lord your God in vain.

4. Remember the Sabbath day and keep it holy.

5. Honor your father and your mother, that your days may be long in the land which the Lord your God gives you.

6. You shall not kill.

7. You shall not commit adultery.

8. You shall not steal.

9. You shall not bear false witness against your neighbor.

10. You shall not covet your neighbor's house; you shall not covet your neighbor's wife, or his manservant, or his maidservant, or his ox, or his ass, or anything that is your neighbor's.

The Ten Commandments became the core of what was later developed and amplified into the Five Books of Moses (the *Pentateuch*). These five books, the first part of the Hebrew scripture (known as the Torah), are often referred to as the Law.

Islam

Although Islam is the youngest of the world's larger religions, it does not consider itself a new tradition but, rather, the culmination of a very old one. Nor does it think of itself as a "religion," if by that word we mean a set of beliefs and actions sealed off from the rest of our worldly business. Islam sees itself as an all-embracing way of life. The two basic sources for the Islamic tradition are the Qur'an (or Koran) and the Hadiths or "traditions" of Muhammad. Upon the death of Muhammad, his faithful scribe and friend, Abu Bekr, became the first Caliph. He began to collect his master's speeches and sermons into a book, called the Koran, which means "The Reading." When the Koran was completed it became a powerful instrument that held Islam together and gave it strength.

Sayings from the Koran

O People! Serve Allah who created you and those who went before you. He made the earth as your resting place and the sky as your canopy; and he sends down rain from heaven to bring forth fruit with which to sustain you. As long as you know this, set up no rivals to Allah!

If you give alms publicly, it is well; but it is better to give them secretly. Allah knows what you do.

Whatever good befalls a man, it is from Allah; whatever ill befalls a man, it is his own doing.

Can the reward of goodness be aught but goodness?

Christianity

The term "Christ" is the English rendering of the Greek *Kristos*, a word used by early Greek-speaking Christians to translate the Hebrew word "mashiah" or "Messiah." Christians everywhere look to the New Testament as a continual source of revelation, inspiration, and renewal, for within its covers is contained what is commonly referred to by Christians as "the greatest story ever told," the story of Jesus of Nazareth. The New Testament records the life and teachings of Jesus. It is also a description of the faith and activity of the early Christians.

The Beatitudes: Matthew 5:3–11

Blessed are the poor in spirit, for theirs is the kingdom
    of heaven.
Blessed are those who mourn, for they shall be comforted.
Blessed are the meek, for they shall inherit the earth.
Blessed are those who hunger and thirst for righteousness,
    for they shall be satisfied.
Blessed are the merciful, for they shall obtain mercy.
Blessed are the pure in heart for they shall see God.
Blessed are the peacemakers, for they shall be called sons
    of God.
Blessed are those who are persecuted for righteousness' sake,
    for theirs is the kingdom of heaven.
Blessed are you when men revile you and persecute you and
    utter all kinds of evil against you falsely on my account.
    Rejoice and be glad, for your reward is great in heaven.

Taoism

The Chinese mind has long beheld the universe as a living process governed by the interplay of opposites. Taoism and Confucianism formed around the same time, around the sixth century B.C. Taoism's beginnings are linked to the legendary figure of Lao-Tzu, senior to Confucius by about fifty years and accredited to writing Taoism's Bible, the *Tao Te Ching* or *Book of the Way and Its Power*.

Some Sayings from the Tao Te Ching

Nameless are the origins of all creation.

The wise man does not teach by words but by deeds.

If you know righteousness, though you die, you shall not perish.

He who humbles himself shall be preserved; he who bends shall be made straight; he who is empty shall be filled; and he who has little shall succeed.

If you work by the Way, you will be of the Way.

Observe all the white around you, but remember all the black that is there.

The wise reject all extremes.

He who understands others is wise; he who understands himself is enlightened.

True compassion is known by its good deeds.

To the good I would be good, and to the bad I would be good; in that way all might become good.

If you see what is small, you have clearness of vision; if you store up small energies, you gain strength.

A thousand-mile journey can be made one step at a time.

Confucianism

The great religions of the world may be divided into three groups of three. The religions that originated in India are Hinduism, Buddhism, and Jainism. The religions that originated in China and Japan are Confucianism, Taoism, and Shinto. And the religions that originated in the Near East are Judaism, Christianity, and Islam. Added to these are other faiths, some ancient and some recent, which offer many other combinations and variations of the three principal groups.

Harmony with the Universal Order

What is God-given is what we call human nature. To fulfill the law of our human nature is what we call the moral law (Tao). The cultivation of the moral law is what we call culture.

The oral law is a law from whose operation we cannot for one instant in our existence escape.

Our central self or moral being is the great basis of existence, and *harmony* or moral order is the universal law in the world.

Confucius remarked: "The life of the moral person is an exemplification of the universal moral order.... The life of the vulgar person, on the other hand, is a contradiction of the universal moral order. To find the central clue to our moral being which unites us to the universal order, that indeed is the highest human attainment."

Six Principles of Confucianism

1. Human nature is good; and evil is essentially unnatural.

2. Man is free to conduct himself as he wills, and he is the master of his choice.

3. Virtue is its own reward. If one does good for a reward, or avoids evil for fear of punishment—that is not virtue.

4. The rule for individual behavior is: what you do not want others to do to you, do not do to them.

5. A man has five duties: to his ruler, to his father, to his wife (and she to him), to his elder brother, to his friend. And the most important of these is the filial duty.

6. Man should strive to become a superior man.

The Five Constant Virtues

When the rulers of the Empire asked Mencius (or Meng Tzu, the second most influential philosopher in the Confucian tradition who lived about a hundred years after his Master) for the essentials of his teachings, he would reply:

1. *Benevolence*, which is always to think first of what is good for the people;

2. *Righteousness*, which is not to do to your subjects what you would not want them to do to you if you were in their place;

3. *Propriety*, which is always to behave with courtesy and respect toward your subjects;

4. *Wisdom*, which is to be guided by knowledge and understanding; and

5. *Sincerity*, which is to be sincere and truthful in all you do.

Buddhism

Buddhism has been called the Light of Asia. In the 2,600 years since that light was kindled in ancient India, it has suffused a wide array of cultures and has been refracted by their palette of indigenous beliefs. Through its many forms, the Buddhist tradition has had a vast influence on the metaphysical imagination, the moral bearing, and the aesthetic sensibility of the diverse peoples of Asia. In the last hundred years it has shown itself to be potentially as fecund for the West.

The Buddha's Final Instructions

"Be Your Own Lamps"

So, Ananda, you must be your own lamps, be your own refuges.... Hold firm to the truth as a lamp and a refuge and do not look for refuge to anything beside yourselves. A monk becomes his own lamp by continually looking on his body, feelings, perceptions, moods, and ideas in such a manner that he conquers the cravings and depressions of ordinary persons and is always diligent, self-possessed, and collected in mind. Whoever among my monks does this, either now or when I am dead, if he is anxious to learn, will reach the summit.

1 Corinthians 13:1–13

If I speak in the tongues of men and of angels,
But have not love,
I am a noisy gong or a clanging cymbal.
And if I have prophetic powers,
And understand all mysteries and all knowledge,
And if I have all faith, so as to remove mountains,
But have not love, I am nothing.
If I give away all I have,
And if I deliver my body to be burned,
But have not love, I gain nothing.

Love is patient and kind;
Love is not jealous or boastful;
It is not arrogant or rude.
Love does not insist upon its own way;
It is not irritable or resentful;
It does not rejoice at wrong,
But rejoices in the right.
Love bears all things,
Believes all things,
Hopes all things,
Endures all things.

Love never ends;
As for prophecies, they will pass away;
As for tongues, they will cease;
As for knowledge, it will pass away.
For our knowledge is imperfect,
And our prophecy is imperfect.
But when the perfect comes,
The imperfect will pass away.
When I was a child, I spoke like a child,

I thought like a child, I reasoned like a child.
When I became a man, I gave up childish ways.
For now we see in a mirror dimly,
But then face to face.
Now I know in part;
Then I shall understand fully,
Even as I have been fully understood.
So faith, hope, love abide, these three;
But the greatest of these is love.

Spirit of the Living God

Spirit of the Living God,
Fall fresh on me.
Spirit of the Living God,
Fall fresh on me.
Melt me, mold me, fill me, use me,
Spirit of the Living God,
Fall fresh on me.
Melt me, mold me, fill me, use me,
Spirit of the Living God,
Fall fresh on me.

  Daniel Iverson

To Worship

To worship is to stand in awe under a heaven of stars,
Before a flower, a leaf in sunlight, or a grain of sand.
To worship is to be silent, receptive,
Before a tree astir with the wind,
Or the passing shadow of a cloud.
To worship is to work with dedication and with skill;
It is to pause from work and listen to a strain of music.
To worship is to sing with the singing beauty of the earth;
It is to listen through a storm to the still small voice within.
Worship is a loneliness seeking communion;
It is a thirsty land crying out for rain.
Worship is kindred fire within our hearts;
It moves through deeds of kindness and through acts of love.
Worship is the mystery within us reaching out to the mystery
   beyond.
It is an articulate silence yearning to speak;
It is the window of the moment open to the sky
   of the eternal.

   Jacob Trapp

The Journey of Love

Where in our hearts is that burning of desire? It is true that we are made of dust and the world is also made of dust, but the dust has motes rising. Whence comes the drive in us? We look to the starry sky and love storms in our hearts. Whence comes that storm? The journey of love is a very long journey, but sometimes with a sign you can cross that vast desert. Search and search again without losing hope. You may find sometime a treasure on your way. My heart and my eyes are all devoted to the vision.

Mohammed Iqbal

The Infinity of God

I see You in all things, O my God. Infinity itself is Your creation. And all around are the signs of Your endlessness: the bursting life of countless plants; the unending song of innumerable birds; the tireless movement of animals and insects. Nowhere can I see a beginning or an end. I see infinite beauty infuse your entire world....

The sun is Your eye during the day, and the moon is Your eye at night. The wind is Your breath, and the fertile earth is Your heart....

As the waters of a river flow to the sea, the path determined by the line of the valley, so we pass through life to death, our destiny mapped out by Your will.

Arjuna

Excerpt from Freedom and Love

Do you know what it means to love somebody? Do you know what it means to love a tree, or a bird, or a pet animal, so that you take care of it, feed it, cherish it, though it may give you nothing in return, though it may not offer you shade, or follow you, or depend on you? Most of us don't love in that way, we don't know what that means at all because our love is always hedged about with anxiety, jealousy, fear—which implies that we depend inwardly on another; we want to be loved. We don't just love and leave it there, but we ask something in return, and in that very asking we become dependent.

So freedom and love go together. Love is not a reaction. If I love you because you love me, that is mere trade, a thing to be bought in the market; it is not love. To love is not to ask anything in return, not even to feel that you are giving something— and it is only such love that can know freedom.

Krishnamurti

A human being is part of a whole, called by us the "Universe," a part limited in time and space. He experiences himself, his thoughts and feelings, as something separated from the rest—a kind of optical delusion of his consciousness. This delusion is a kind of prison for us, restricting us to our personal desires and to affection for a few persons nearest us. Our task must be to free ourselves from this prison by widening our circles of compassion to embrace all living creatures and the whole of nature in its beauty.

Albert Einstein

The practice of mindfulness unveils and reveals your essential Good Heart, because it dissolves and removes the unkindness or the harm in you. Only when you have removed the harm in yourself do you become truly useful to others. Through the practice, by slowly removing the unkindness and harm from yourself, you allow your true Good Heart, the fundamental goodness and kindness that are your real nature, to shine out and become the warm climate in which your true being flowers.

Sogyal Rinpoche

We should seek to benefit from the inspiring highlights of other denominations and religions, not just to tolerate them. We should try our very best to give the beauties of our religion to others, because sharing our most prized possessions is the highest form of "Love thy neighbor." Let us not water down the diverse religions into a know-nothing soup; but rather let us study enthusiastically the glorious highlights of each. An old Chinese precept is, "The good man does not grieve that other people do not recognize his merits. His only anxiety is lest he should fail to recognize theirs." It is a mistake for people of different religions to try to agree with each other. The result is not the best of each but rather the watered-down, least-common denominator. What is more fruitful is a spirit of humility in which we recognize that no one will ever comprehend all that God is. Therefore, let us permit and encourage each prophet to proclaim the best as it is revealed to him. There is no conflict unless the restrictive idea of exclusiveness enters in. We can hold our ideas of the Gospel with the utmost enthusiasm, while humbly admitting that we know ever so little of the whole and that there is plenty of room for those who think they have seen God in a different way. The evil arises only if one prophet forbids his audience to listen to any other prophet. The conceit and self-centeredness of such restriction—the false pride of saying that God can be only what we have learned Him to be—should be obvious....

It appears that God's creative method is movement, change, continuing search, ongoing inquiry. Those who seek are rewarded. Those who are sure they already have the answers gradually become obsolete. Perhaps "built-in" obsolescence is God's plan for keeping the world of ideas forever young, fresh, and invigorating. The self-confident proud grow old and die, and with them die their ideas.

John Marks Templeton

Excerpt from The Wholeness of Life

Most of us cling to some small part of life, and think that through that part we shall discover the whole. Without leaving the room we hope to explore the whole length and width of the river and perceive the richness of the green pastures along its banks. We live in a little room, we paint on a little canvas, thinking that we have grasped life by the hand or understood the significance of death; but we have not. To do that we must go outside. And it is extraordinarily difficult to go outside, to leave the room with its narrow window and see everything as it is without judging, without condemning, without saying, "This I like and that I don't like"; because most of us think that through the part we shall understand the whole. Through a single spoke we hope to understand the wheel; but one spoke does not make a wheel, does it? It takes many spokes, as well as a hub and a rim, to make the thing called a wheel, and we need to see the whole wheel in order to comprehend it. In the same way we must perceive the whole process of living if we are really to understand life....

Life is an extraordinary mystery—not the mystery in books, not the mystery that people talk about, but a mystery that one has to discover for oneself; and that is why it is so grave a matter that you should understand the little, the narrow, the petty, and go beyond it.

... That is why it is very important to leave your little room and perceive the whole expanse of the heavens. But you cannot do that unless you have love—not bodily love or divine love, but just love; which is to love the birds, the trees, the flowers, your teachers, your parents, and beyond your parents, humanity.

Krishnamurti

A Smile Is an Investment

Most people feel intuitively that the simplest things in life are the most important, or, if you prefer, that the most important things in life are found to be the simplest. This is a very profound discovery. What is more important to us than breathing, for instance?—yet we seldom give it a thought—fresh air doesn't cost a penny—and if deprived of air we die in a few minutes.

Another simple thing which is of great moment is a *smile!* A smile costs nothing in money, time, or effort, but it is literally true that it can be of supreme importance in one's life. A smile affects your whole body from the skin right in to the skeleton, including all blood vessels, nerves, and muscles. It affects the functioning of every organ. It influences every gland. I repeat—and this is literally true—you cannot smile without affecting your whole body favorably. Even one smile often relaxes quite a number of muscles, and when the thing becomes a habit, you can easily see how the effect will mount up. *Last year's smiles are paying you dividends today.*

The effect of a smile on other people is no less remarkable. It disarms suspicion, melts away fear and anger, and brings forth the best in the other person—which best he immediately proceeds to give to you.

A smile is to personal contacts what oil is to machinery, and no intelligent engineer ever neglects lubrication.

Emmet Fox

Thoughts on Love: Luke 6:27–38

But I say to you that hear, love your enemies, do good to those who hate you, bless those who curse you, pray for those who abuse you. To him who strikes you on the cheek, offer the other also; and from him who takes away your cloak do not withhold your coat as well. Give to every one who begs from you; and of him who takes away your goods do not ask them again. And as you wish that men would do to you, do so to them.

If you love those who love you, what credit is that to you? For even sinners love those who love them. And if you do good to those who do that to you, what credit is that to you? For even sinners do the same. And if you lend to those from whom you hope to receive, what credit is that to you? Even sinners lend to sinners, to receive as much again. But love your enemies, and do good, and lend, expecting nothing in return and your reward will be great, and you will be sons of the Most High; for He is kind to the ungrateful and the selfish. Be merciful, even as your Father is merciful.

Judge not, and you will not be judged; condemn not, and you will not be condemned; forgive, and you will be forgiven; give, and it will be given unto you; good measure, pressed down, shaken together, running over, will be put into your lap. For the measure you give will be the measure you get back.

The Supreme Fact of the Universe

The great central fact of the universe is that Spirit of Infinite Life and Power that is back of all, that animates all, that manifests itself in and through all; that self-existent principle of life from which all has come, and not only from which all has come, but from which all is continually coming. If there is an individual life, there must of necessity be an infinite source of life from which it comes. If there is a quality or a force of love, there must of necessity be an infinite source of love whence it comes. If there is wisdom, there must be the all-wise source back of it from which it springs. The same is true in regard to peace, the same in regard to power, the same in regard to what we call material things.

There is, then, this Spirit of Infinite Life and Power back of all which is the source of all. This Infinite Power is creating, working, ruling through the agency of great immutable laws and forces that run through all the universe, that surround us on every side....

In a sense there is nothing in all the great universe but law. If this is true there must of necessity be a force behind it all that is the maker of these laws and a force greater than the laws that are made. This Spirit of Infinite Life and Power that is back of all is what I call God....

God, then, is this Infinite Spirit which fills all the universe with Himself alone, so that all is from Him and in Him, and there is nothing that is outside. Indeed and in truth, then, in Him we live and move and have our being. He is the life of our life, our very life itself.

Ralph Waldo Trine

The Supreme Fact of Human Life

From the great central fact of the universe in regard to which we have agreed, namely, this Spirit of Infinite Life that is back of all and from which all comes, we are led to inquire as to what is the great central fact in human life. From what has gone before, the question almost answers itself.

The great central face in human life, in your life and in mine, is the coming into a conscious, vital realization of our oneness with this Infinite Life, and the opening of ourselves fully to this divine flow.

This is the great central fact in human life, for in this all else is included, all else follows in its train. In just the degree that we come into a conscious realization of our oneness with the Infinite Life and open ourselves to this divine inflow, do we actualize in ourselves the qualities and powers of the Infinite Life.

And what does this mean? It means simply this: that we are recognizing our true identity, that we are bringing our lives into harmony with the same great laws and forces, and so opening ourselves to the same great aspirations as have all the prophets, seers, sages, and saviors in the world's history, all men of truly great and mighty power. For in the degree that we come into this realization and connect ourselves with this Infinite Source, do we make it possible for the higher powers to play, to work, to manifest through us.

Ralph Waldo Trine

Humility

At this present moment, the human race, even after thousands of years of historical development, is still at the dawn of a new creation. This is a tremendous, awe-inspiring responsibility. It should humble us.

In fact, humility is the key to progress. Without it we will be too self-satisfied with past glories to launch boldly into the challenges ahead. Without humility we will not be wide-eyed and open-minded enough to discover new areas for research. If we are not as humble as children, we may be unable to admit mistakes, seek advice, and try again. The humble approach is for all of us who are concerned about the future of our civilization and the role we are to play in it. It is an approach for all of us who are not satisfied to let things drift and who want to channel our creative restlessness toward helping to build the kingdom of God.

Every person's concept of God is too small. Through humility we can begin to get into true perspective the infinity of God. This is the humble approach.

It is also in humility that we learn from each other, for it makes us open to each other and ready to see things from the other's point of view and share ours with him freely. It is by humility that we avoid the sins of pride and intolerance and avoid all religious strife. Humility opens the door to the realms of spirit, and to research and progress in religion.

John Marks Templeton

Be Like a Child

Be like a child; look at thy two feet and say, Lord, walk these for me. Talk to him as to thy friend and nurse. Be in sweet communion friendship with him. Call him in thy bath, in thy daily tasks, in thy going from one room to another. Say, Nay, I will not go alone. Come, be thou with me, lead thou the way. Behold, he will answer then, and come running like laughter and golden hope into thy heart, and with understanding love will he walk with thee from room to room. And, too, will he stand beside thee when thou faceth thy friends and visitors, and he will place a hand in thine and will watch thy heart and the issues therefrom so that thou canst talk in perfect safety knowing that thy word will be food and drink and life to all in thy presence.

For thou hast him all to thyself. He is thine—forever. Do not puzzle how he can see thy two feet when there are millions of feet, that is too much for thine understanding. Enough that it is the truth that he hath never failed to come when called and that he will come as thou dost want him. He is to be sought through the refinements of the heart. Go, then, and ask him to rest thee, to heal thy complaints, and to fill thee with the strong virtue required. He will manifest, he never faileth. He is thy Saviour and sweet comforter. So go into thy immediate and personal life with him for thy very own, with thy hand in his. Let him smooth thy pillow, smooth thy blanket; and in deep, loosened sleep let him teach thee that the Life immortal, perfect divine Sonship with him, can be known in all its fullness by such a simple way as this childlike invitation to him—the eternal Guest.

from Letters of the Scattered Brotherhood

All Spiritual Invitations Come from the Same Host

Place your devotion whole-heartedly at the service of the ideal most natural to your being, but know with unwavering certainty that all spiritual ideals are expressions of the same supreme Presence. Do not allow the slightest trace of malice to enter your mind toward any manifestation of God or toward any practitioner who attempts to live in harmony with that Divine Manifestation. Kali, Krishna, Buddha, Christ, Allah—these are all full expressions of the same indivisible Consciousness and Bliss. These are revelatory initiatives of Divine Reality, not manmade notions. Blessed is the soul who has known that all is one, that all jackals howl essentially alike.

Ramakrishna, The Bhagavad Gita

May beings all live happily and safe
And may their hearts rejoice within themselves.
Whatever there may be with breath of life,
Whether they be frail or very strong,
Without exception, be they long or short,
Or middle-sized, or be they big or small,
Or thick, or visible, or invisible,
Or whether they dwell far or they dwell near,
Those that are here, those seeking to exist—
May all beings all rejoice within themselves.
Let no one bring about another's ruin
And not despise in any way or place,
Let them not wish each other any ill
From provocation or from enmity.

The Buddha, from the Sutta Nipata

Psalm 133

Behold, how good and pleasant it is when brothers
    dwell in unity!
It is like the precious oil upon the head, running down
    upon the beard,
Upon the beard of Aaron, running down on the collar
    of his robes!
It is like the dew of Hermon, which falls on the mountains
    of Zion!
For there the Lord has commanded the blessing,
Life forevermore.

There is in all things an inexhaustible sweetness and purity, a silence that is a fount of action and joy. It rises up in wordless gentleness and flows out to me from the unseen roots of all created being, welcoming me tenderly, saluting me with indescribable humility.

Thomas Merton

He who has a thousand friends
   has not a friend to spare.
And he who has one enemy will
   meet him everywhere.

'Ali

Atman: The Universal Self

Death: Atman, the spirit of vision is never born and never dies. Before him there was nothing, and he is ONE forevermore. Never-born and eternal, beyond times gone or to come, he does not die when the body dies.

If the slayer thinks that he kills, and if the slain thinks that he dies, neither knows the way of Truth. The Eternal in man cannot kill; the Eternal in man cannot die.

Concealed in the heart of all beings is the Atman. The Spirit, the Self; smaller than the smallest atom, greater than the vast spaces. The man who surrenders his human will leaves sorrows behind, and beholds the glory of the Atman by the grace of the Creator.... Not even through deep knowledge can the Atman be reached, unless evil ways are abandoned, and there is rest in the senses, concentration in the mind, and peace in one's heart.

The Upanishads

In this section, Death is the speaker
and continues his teaching to Nachiketas.

See All Beings in Your Own Self
and Your Self in All Beings

Behold the universe in the glory of God; and all that lives and moves on earth. Leaving the transient, find joy in the Eternal; set not your heart on another's possessions....

The Spirit, without moving, is swifter than the mind; the senses cannot reach him. He is ever beyond them. Standing still, he overtakes those who run. To the ocean of his being, the spirit of life leads the streams of action.

... Who sees all beings in his own Self, and his own Self in all beings, loses all fear.

... When a sage sees this great Unity and his Self has become all beings, what delusion and what sorrow can ever be near him?

... May life go to immortal life, and the body go to ashes. OM. Oh my soul, remember past strivings, remember! O my soul, remember past strivings, remember!

Isa Upanishad

The nineteenth-century German philosopher Arthur Schopenhauer paid homage to the sublime ideas that have been animating the Hindu tradition for years when he said, "In the whole world, there is no study so beautiful and so elevating as the Upanishads."

O All-Transcendent God
(What other name describes you?)

What words can sing your praises
    No word at all denotes you.
What mind can probe your secret?
    No mind at all can grasp you,
Alone beyond the power of speech,
    all men can speak of springs from you;
alone beyond the power of thought,
    all men can think of stems from you.
All things proclaim you—
    things that can speak, things that cannot.
All things revere you—
    Things that have reason, things that have none.
The whole world's longing
    and pain mingle about you.
All things breathe you a prayer,
    a silent hymn of your own composing.
All that exists you uphold,
    All things in concert move to your orders.
You are the end of all that is,
    you are one, you are all;
you are none of the things that are,
    you are not a part and not the whole.
All names are at your disposal;
    how shall I name you, the only unnameable?
What mind's affinities with heaven
    Can pierce the veils above the clouds?
Mercy, all-transcendent God
    (What other name describes you?)

    Saint Gregory Nazianzus

Earth Teach Me to Remember

Earth teach me stillness
    as the grasses are stilled with light.
Earth teach me suffering
    as old stones suffer with memory.
Earth teach me humility
    as blossoms are humble with beginning.
Earth teach me caring
    as the mother who secures her young.
Earth teach me courage
    as the tree which stands alone.
Earth teach me limitation
    as the ant who crawls on the ground.
Earth teach me freedom
    as the eagle which soars in the sky.
Earth teach me resignation
    as the leaves which die in the fall.
Earth teach me regeneration
    as the seed which rises in the spring.
Earth teach me to forget myself
    as melted snow forgets its life.
Earth teach me to remember kindness
    as dry fields weep with rain.

Ute (North America)

Psalm 104:5–15

God established the earth on its foundations,
so that it shall never totter.
You made the deep cover it as a garment;
    the waters stood above the mountains....
Mountains rising, valleys sinking—
    to the place you established for them.
You make springs gush forth torrents;
    they make their way between the hills,
Giving drink to all the wild beasts;
    the wild asses slake their thirst.
The birds of the sky dwell beside them
    and sing among the foliage . . .
You make the grass grow for the cattle,
    and herbage for human labor
    that we may get food out of the earth—
Wine that cheers human hearts,
    oil that makes the face shine,
    and bread that sustains our life.

Lord, Make Me an Instrument of Thy Peace

Lord, make me an instrument of Thy peace.
Where there is hatred, let me sow love,
Where there is offense, pardon,
Where there is discord, unity,
Where there is doubt, faith,
Where there is error, truth,
Where there is despair, hope,
Where there is sadness, joy,
Where there is darkness, light.
   Oh, Divine Master, grant that I may not so much seek
To be consoled as to console.
To be understood as to understand,
To be loved as to love.
   For:
It is in giving that we receive.
It is in pardoning that we are pardoned.
It is in dying that we are born to eternal life.

Saint Francis of Assisi

The Path of Love

1. Remember your soul and follow your heart. It takes courage to act on motivations of love rather than fear. The stronger you feel, the softer and more vulnerable you can allow yourself to be. The more fearful you are, the more you think you have to defend yourself against potential dangers and scare people away in order to be safe. But no armor can keep fear out of your heart. Only a willingness to look deeper, to face the fear that lurks in the shadows can make illusions vanish like a dream.
2. Invite love into your life. Intend to be loving and accept being loved. Open to the abundance of mutual exchange available in loving relationships without self-sacrifice.
3. Notice how you resist or avoid love. Welcome the tears and laughter that express love.
4. Love yourself and others equally, not more or less. Love is kind. Be kind to yourself and to all beings. Ask yourself how you could love yourself and others better.
5. Learn to see love and beauty in the world. Love the beauty inside yourself and other people as much as the beauty of nature, light, color, and sound perceived by the physical senses. Inner beauty's perceived with the eye of the soul.
6. Love the joy of being wherever you are as much as you can, growing into clear awareness.
7. Remember love is ever present, here, now, and always.
   > Identify with love, and you are safe.
   > Identify with love, and you are home.
   > Identify with love, and find your Self.

from A Course in Miracles

What Is Contemplation?

Contemplation is spontaneous awe at the sacredness of life.... It is gratitude for life, for awareness and for being. It is a vivid realization of the fact that life and being proceed from an invisible, transcendent and infinitely abundant Source.

Thomas Merton

How to Awaken Love and Compassion

When we believe that we don't have enough love in us, there is a method for discovering and invoking it. Go back in your mind and recreate, almost visualize, a love that someone gave you that really moved you, perhaps in your childhood.... Now let that feeling arise again in your heart, and infuse you with gratitude. As you do so, your love will go out naturally to that person who evoked it. You will remember then that even though you may not always feel that you have been loved enough, you were loved genuinely once. Knowing that now will make you feel again that you are, as that person made you feel then, worthy of love and really lovable.

Let your heart open now, and let love flow from it; then extend this love to all beings. Begin with those who are closest to you, then extend your love to friends and to acquaintances, then to neighbors, to strangers, then even to those whom you don't like or have difficulties with, even those whom you might consider as your "enemies," and finally to the whole universe. Let this love become more and more boundless. Equanimity is one of the four essential facets, with loving kindness, compassion, and joy, of what the teachings say form the entire aspiration of compassion. The all-inclusive, unbiased view of equanimity is really the starting point and the basis of the path of compassion.

Sogyal Rinpoche

Keep on the Beam

Today most commercial flying is done on a radio beam. A directional beam is produced to guide the pilot to his destination, and as long as he keeps on this beam he knows that he is safe, even if he cannot see around him for fog, or get his bearings in any other way.

As soon as he gets off the beam in any direction he is in danger, and he immediately tries to get back on the beam once more.

Those who believe in the All-ness of God have a spiritual beam upon which to navigate on the voyage of life.

As long as you have peace of mind and some sense of the Presence of God you are on the beam, and you are safe, even if outer things seem to be confused or even very dark; but as soon as you get off the beam, you are in danger.

You are off the beam the moment you are *angry* or *resentful* or *jealous* or *frightened* or *depressed*; and when such a condition arises you should immediately get back on the beam by turning quietly to God in thought, claiming His Presence, claiming that His Love and Intelligence are with you, and that the promises in the Bible are true today. If you do this you are back on the beam, even if outer conditions and your own feelings do not change immediately. You are safe on the beam and you will reach port in safety.

Keep on the beam and nothing shall by any means hurt you.

Emmet Fox

Amor Dei

Give me to be Thy child, and learn forever at Thy knee.
Give me to grow weak and grey-headed, since Thou willst it so.
Bid me aside
Lay all the pleasures of my youth and pride,
Gladness as well,
Sweet ardours and bright hopes—I'll not rebel.

Only, I pray, keep me beside Thee all the night and day.
Only for all Thou takest give Thyself and past recall!
And when youth's gone
As men count going, twixt us two alone
Still let me be
Thy little child, left learning at Thy knee.

Anonymous

There is nothing I can give you
which you do have not;
But there is much, very much, that
while I cannot give it, you can take.

No heaven can come to us unless our hearts
find rest in today. Take heaven!
No peace lies in the future which is not hidden
in this present instant. Take peace!

The gloom of the world is but a shadow.
Behind it, yet within reach, is joy.
There is a radiance and glory in the darkness,
    could we but see,
and to see, we have only to look. I beseech you to look.

Fra Giovanni

Finding God in Our Work

God does not deflect our gaze prematurely from the work He Himself has given us, since He presents Himself to us as attainable through that very work. Nor does He blot out, in His intense light, the detail of our earthly aims, since the closeness of our union with Him is in fact determined by the exact fulfillment of the least of our tasks.... God, in all that is most living and incarnate in Him, is not far away from us, altogether apart from the world we see, touch, hear, smell, and taste about us. Rather He awaits us every instant in our action, in the work of the moment. There is a sense in which He is at the tip of my pen, my spade, my brush, my needle—of my heart and of my thought. By pressing the stroke, the line, or the stitch, on which I am engaged, to its ultimate natural finish, I shall lay hold of the last end towards which my innermost will tends.... Try, with God's help, to perceive the connection—even physical and natural—which binds your labour with the building of the Kingdom of Heaven; try to realise that heaven itself smiles upon you and, through your works, draws you to itself; then, as you leave church for the noisy streets, you will remain with only one feeling, that of continuing to immerse yourself in God.... Never, at any time ... consent to do anything without first of all realising its significance and constructive value in Christo Jesu, and pursuing it with all your might. This is not simply a commonplace precept for salvation: it is the very path to sanctity for each man according to his state and calling. For what is sanctity in a creature if not to adhere to God with the maximum of his strength? —and what does that maximum adherence to God mean if not the fulfillment—in the world organized around Christ—of the exact function, be it lowly or eminent, to which that creature is destined both by natural endowment and by supernatural gift?

Pierre Teilhard de Chardin

Das Energi

God is what is there when you take away the distance.

All human consciousness is moving towards this awareness.
No field of human endeavor will fail to be revolutionized by it.
We're all going to meet in the present.

Everybody wants to know,
    What can I do? We all want to save the planet, pick up the
    garbage, free our brothers and sisters, stop war and bring the
    millennium
        but what can I do, seriously?

Okay, seriously:
  get to reality,
      get to your own reality,
         become yourself,
become incredibly high and real and influence
everyone around you with your vibrations.
      no matter how difficult it is,
         drop everything else and
         start doing the most fantastic, real things you can think of—
become yourself
get to your own reality . . .

take everything that is strong in you
      and put it to work
         set it free
    never mind what anyone thinks.
take all your muscles
      and stretch them to their limits

you'll amaze yourself, how good you'll feel
    and how much good you'll do
just by radiating pure energy outward.
—contact high the ultimate form of communication—
    You are beautiful.
        Be.
        Be.
        Be.

    Paul Williams

My whole being pulsates
   with the fire of desire
      for our everlasting union.
My very breath is but Yours.
   My heart is a limitless beacon
      of Your Love.

My spirit, being Yours,
   is the light of the world.
        My eyes but radiate and reflect
        our Perfect Love.
My very essence vibrates with You
   as the harmony of music
      not yet heard.

My vision is but Your Love
   flowing through me,
      seeing only its own reflection.
My only fulfillment is following Your
   directions and guidance.

My voice, being Yours,
   can only bless.
My prayer is but an eternal song of gratitude,
   that You are in me,
      and I am in You.
And that I live in Your Grace
   forever.

     Gerald G. Jampolsky

Father Reason

The universe is a form of divine law,
your reasonable father.

When you feel ungrateful to him,
the shapes of the world seem mean and ugly.

Make peace with that father, the elegant patterning,
and every experience will fill with immediacy.

Because I love this, I am never bored.
Beauty constantly wells up, a noise of springwater
in my ear and in my inner being.

Tree limbs rise and fall like the ecstatic arms
of those who have submitted to the mystical life.

Leaf sounds talk together like poets
making fresh metaphors. The green felt cover slips,
and we get a flash of the mirror underneath.

Think how it will be when the whole thing
is pulled away! I tell only one one-thousandth
of what I see, because there's so much doubt everywhere.

The conventional opinion of this poetry is,
it shows great optimism for the future.

But Father Reason says,
No need to announce the future!
This now is it. *This.* Your deepest need and desire
is satisfied by the *moment's* energy
here in your hand.

> *Rumi. Translated by Coleman Barks.*

Psalm 19:1–6

The heavens are telling the glory of God.
And the firmament proclaims His handiwork.
Day to day pours forth speech,
And night to night declares knowledge.
There is no speech, nor are there words;
Their voice is not heard;
Yet their voice goes out through all the earth,
And their words to the end of the world.
In them he has set a tent for the sun,
Which comes forth like a bridegroom leaving his chamber,
And like a strong man runs its course with joy.
Its rising is from the end of the heavens,
And its circuit to the end of them;
And there is nothing hid from its heart.

Excerpt from "Orderly Thinking"

But happiness is not something that you can seek; it is a result, a by-product. If you pursue happiness for itself it will have no meaning. Happiness comes uninvited; and the moment you are conscious that you are happy, you are no longer happy. I wonder if you have noticed this? When you are suddenly joyous about nothing in particular, there is just the freedom of smiling, of being happy; but, the moment you are conscious of it, you have lost it, have you not? Being self-consciously happy, or pursuing happiness, is the very ending of happiness. There is happiness only when the self and its demands are put aside.

   Krishnamurti

Sensitivity

Now, what does it mean to be sensitive. To be cognizant of color and form, of what people say and of your response to it; to be considerate, to have good taste, good manners; not to be rough, not to hurt people either physically or inwardly and be unaware of it; to see a beautiful thing and linger with it; to listen tentatively without being bored to everything that is said, so that the mind becomes acute, sharp—all this is sensitivity, is it not? So is there much difference between sensitivity and awareness? I don't think so.

   Krishnamurti

Only Breath

Not Christian or Jew or Muslim, not Hindu,
Buddhist, sufi, or zen. Not any religion

or cultural system. I am not from the East
or the West, not out of the ocean or up

from the ground, not natural or ethereal, not
composed of elements at all. I do not exist,

am not an entity in this world or the next,
did not descend from Adam and Eve or any

origin story. My place is placeless, a trace
of the traceless. Neither body or soul

I belong to the beloved, have seen the two
worlds as one and that one call to and know,

first, last, outer, inner, only that
breath breathing human being.

    Rumi

In your light I learn how to love.
In your beauty, how to make poems.

You dance inside my chest,
where no one sees you,

but sometimes I do,
and that sight becomes this art.

   Rumi

Love

When love is truly responsible, it is one's duty to love all men. Man has no choice but to accept this duty, for when he does not, he finds his alternatives lie in loneliness, destruction, and despair. To assume this responsibility is for him to become involved in delight, in mystery and growth. It is to dedicate himself to the process of helping others to realize their love through him. Simply speaking, to be responsible in love is to help other men to love. To be helped toward realizing your love is to be loved by other men.

Men have been known to approach this responsibility to love from different means, but the ends are always the same, universal love. Some begin with a deep personal involvement with another individual. From this, they learn that love cannot be exclusive. They learn that if love is to grow, it will need diverse minds, innumerable individuals, and the exploration of varied paths. No one human being can afford him all these things, so he must enlarge his love to include all mankind in his love. The more all-encompassing his love, the greater his growth. The love of humanity is the natural outgrowth of love for a single individual. From one man to all men.

Leo Buscaglia

The Desiderata

Go placidly amid the noise and haste and remember what peace there may be in silence.

As far as possible, without surrender, be on good terms with all persons. Speak your truth quietly and clearly and listen to others, even the dull and ignorant; they, too, have their story.

Avoid loud and aggressive persons; they are vexations to the spirit. If you compare yourself with others, you may become vain and bitter for always there will be greater and lesser persons than yourself. Enjoy your achievements as well as your plans.

Keep interested in your own career, however humble; it is a real possession in the changing fortunes of time. Exercise caution in your business affairs, for the world is full of trickery. But let this not blind you to what virtue there is. Many persons strive for high ideals; and everywhere life is full of heroism.

Be yourself. Especially, do not feign affection. Neither be cynical about love; for in the face of all aridity and disenchantment it is perennial as grass.

Take kindly the counsel of the years, gracefully surrendering the things of youth. Nurture strength of spirit to shield you in sudden misfortune. But do not distress yourself with imaginings. Many fears are born of fatigue and loneliness. Beyond a wholesome discipline, be gentle with yourself.

You are a child of the universe, no less than the trees and the stars; you have a right to be here. And whether or not it is clear to you, no doubt the universe is unfolding as it should.

Therefore be at peace with God, whatever you conceive Him to be, and whatever your labors and aspirations, in the noisy confusion of life, keep peace with your soul.

With all its sham, drudgery, and broken dreams, it is still a beautiful world. Be cheerful. Strive to be happy.

Max Ehrmann

❧

Excerpt from the Bhagavad Gita

Freedom from fear, purity of heart, constancy in sacred learning and contemplation, generosity, self-harmony, adoration, study of the scriptures, austerity, righteousness;

Nonviolence, truth, freedom from anger, renunciation, serenity, aversion to fault-finding, sympathy for all beings, peace from greedy cravings, gentleness, modesty, steadiness;

Energy, forgiveness, fortitude, purity, a good will, freedom from pride—these are the treasures of the man who is born for heaven.

Deceitfulness, insolence and self-conceit, anger and harshness, and ignorance—these belong to a man who is born for hell.

God Be in My Head

God be in my head, and in my understanding;
God be in my eyes, and in my looking;
God be in my mouth, and in my speaking;
God be in my heart, and in my thinking;
God be at my end, and at my departing.

The Path of Love

Love is a dynamic and inspiring throbbing of the heart. Love is the very nature of God, whom the scriptural authors have called supreme Bliss, and Satchidananda. It exists in its fullness within man. Even if he does not experience it, it is nonetheless there. A blind man who has never seen the light may say when he hears others talk about it, "There is no light. I have never seen it. I don't know anything about it." Yet the light exists; it is only that he has no eyes. Similarly there is love, whether or not it is experienced. If you have not followed the path of love, if you have not tried to find it, how can it be attained?

Love is nectar. Love is immortal. Through love alone, the *gopis* of Gokul found God. Love is a glimpse of the secret inner cave. Love that dwells within flows out through the different sense organs. When it flows to the eyes, it makes forms beautiful; when it flows to the ears, it makes sounds melodious; when it rises to the tongue, it makes tastes sweet and pleasing....

In your ordinary life, learn to love. This love should be pure, unattached, and given for its own sake. If it contains any demands, it is just a commercial exchange—the motions of love, but not love itself. Real love contains no demands, no "mine and yours," no selfishness. Love is just love.... There is enough love in the human heart for not just one man but for thousands, but because of desire and useless thinking, an unfortunate person cannot see it. Once he becomes free of these, he discovers pure, immortal, and complete love.

To find love you must first of all love yourself.

Muktananda

Fundamentals

A rich world lies before us, wide vistas, great depths, infinite boundless, unquestionable light. Plunge, O Man, into the depths of your heart to these currents of light and of life. Live! Live in every atom of your being! Live and you will see that there is still room for love, for faith, for idealism, for creation; and perhaps, who knows, there may yet be worlds still undreamed of.

A. D. Gordon

Naked a man comes into the world, and naked he leaves it; after all his toil, he carries away nothing—except the deeds he leaves behind.

Adapted from Rashi

At the Turning

Existence will remain meaningless for you if you yourself do not penetrate into it with active love and if you do not in this way discover its meaning for yourself. Everything is waiting to be hallowed by you; it is waiting for this meaning to be disclosed and to be realized by you.... Meet the world with the fullness of your being and you shall meet God. If you wish to believe, love!

Martin Buber

A great Hasidic rabbi, Rabbi Zisye was on his deathbed, surrounded by his family and students. Suddenly he began to cry. The students asked him why he was crying. He replied that he was thinking of his appearance before the heavenly court and how he would justify his life. "If I am asked," he told them, "'Why were you not as great as Abraham?' I will have an easy answer. 'I was not born with Abraham's intellectual abilities.' If I am asked, 'Rabbi, why were you not as great as Moses?' I will also have an easy answer. 'I was not born with his leadership abilities.' But if I am asked, 'Why were you not as great as Zisye could have been?' for that I will have no answer!"

Psalm 1:1–3

Blessed are the man and woman
   who have grown beyond their greed
   and who have put an end to their hatred
   and no longer nourish illusions.
But they delight in the way things are
   and keep their hearts open, day and night.
They are like trees planted near flowing rivers,
   which bear fruit when they are ready.
Their leaves will not fall or wither.
   Everything they do will succeed.

    Translated by Stephen Mitchell

In Praise of Wisdom: Wisdom 7:24–30

For wisdom is more active than all active thoughts; and reacheth everywhere by reason of her purity.

For she is a vapor of the power of God, and a certain pure emanation of the glory of the almighty God: and therefore no defiled thing cometh into her.

For she is the brightness of eternal light, and the unspotted mirror of God's majesty, and the image of his goodness.

And being but one, she can do all things: and remaining in herself the same, she reneweth all things, and through nations conveyeth herself into holy sounds, she maketh the friends of God and prophets...

For she is more beautiful than the sun, and above all the order of the stars: being compared with the light, she is found before it.

For after this cometh night, but no evil can overcome wisdom.

In this beautiful passage from the apocryphal Book of Wisdom, the virtue of holy wisdom is personified as being something akin to a breath from God, a sacred and undefiled force that prevails over every evil and inspires holy souls in every generation.

Philippians 4:8

Whatever is true,
Whatever is honorable,
Whatever is just,
Whatever is pure,
Whatever is lovely,
Whatever is gracious,
If there is any excellence,
If there is anything worthy of praise,
Think about these things.

The Sacred Hoop

Then I was standing on the highest mountain of them all, and round beneath me was the whole hoop of the world. And while I stood there I saw more than I can tell and I understood more than I saw. For I was seeing in the sacred manner the shape of all things of the spirit. And the shapes as they must live together like one being. And I saw that the sacred hoop of my people was one of many hoops that make one circle, wide as daylight and starlight, and in the center grew one mighty flowering tree to shelter all the children of one mother and one father. And I saw that it was holy.

Black Elk

My contemplation of life and human nature in that secluded place (cell 54 of Cairo Central Prison) taught me that he who cannot change the very fabric of his thought will never, therefore, make any progress.

Anwar Sadat

A wave in the sea, seen in one way, seems to have a distinct identity, an end and a beginning, a birth and a death. Seen in another way, the wave itself doesn't really exist but is just the behavior of water, "empty" of any separate identity but "full" of water. So when you really think about the wave, you come to realize that it is something that has been made temporarily possible by wind and water, and is dependent on a set of constantly changing circumstances. You also realize that every wave is related to every other wave.

Sogyal Rinpoche

Four things support the world: the learning of the wise, the justice of the great, the prayers of the good, and the valor of the brave.

Muhammad

The Way

Friend, I have lost the way.
    The way leads on.
Is there another way?
    The way is one.
I must retrace the track.
    It's lost and gone.
Back, I must travel back!
    None goes there, none.
Then I'll make here my place—
    The road runs on—
Stand still and set my face—
    The road leaps on.
Stay here, forever stay.
    None stays here, none.
I cannot find the way.
    The way leads on.
Oh, places I have passed!
    That journey's done.
And what will come at last?
    The way leads on.

    Edwin Muir

The Future of Man

Gloriously situated by life at this critical point in the evolution of mankind, what ought we to do? We hold Earth's future in our hands. What shall we decide? In my view the road to be followed is clearly revealed by teaching of all the past.

We can progress only by uniting: this, as we have seen, is the law of life. But unification through coercion leads only to a superficial pseudo-unity. It may establish a mechanism, but it does not achieve any fundamental synthesis; and in consequence it engenders no growth of consciousness. It materializes, in short, instead of spiritualising. Only unification through unanimity is biologically valid. This alone can work the miracle of causing heightened personality to emerge from the forces of collectivity. It alone represents a genuine extension of the psychogenesis that gave us birth.

Therefore it is inwardly that we must come together, and in entire freedom. But this brings us to the last question of all. To create this unanimity we need the bond, as I said, the cement of a favoring influence. Where shall we look for it; how shall we conceive of this principle of togetherness, this soul of the Earth?

Is it to be in the development of a common *vision*, that is to say, the establishment of a universally accepted body of knowledge, in which all intelligences will join in knowing the same facts interpreted in the same way?

Or will it rather be in common *action*, in the determination of an objective universally recognized as being so desirable that all activity will naturally converge towards it under the impulse of a common fear and a common ambition?

These two kinds of unanimity are undoubtedly real, and will, I believe, have their place in our future progress.

Pierre Teilhard de Chardin

The Meaning of the Sacred Pipe

With this sacred pipe you will walk upon the Earth; for the Earth is your Grandmother and Mother, and She is sacred. Every step that is taken upon Her should be as a prayer. The bowl of this pipe is of red stone; it is the Earth. Carved in the stone and facing the center is this buffalo calf who represents all the four-leggeds who live upon your Mother. The stem of the pipe is of wood, and this represents all that grows upon the Earth. And these twelve feathers which hang here where the stem fits into the bowl ... represent the eagle and all the wingeds of the air. All these peoples, and all the things of the universe, are joined to you who smoke the pipe—all send their voices to *Wakan-Tanka*, the Great Spirit. When you pray with this pipe, you pray for and with everything.

Black Elk

In this writing, Black Elk, seer of the Oglala Sioux, recalls the instructions given by the White Buffalo Cow Woman, who in primeval times brought the calumet (sacred pipe) to human beings.

Love courses through everything,
No, Love *is* everything.
How can you say, *there is no love,*
   When nothing but Love exists?
All that you see has appeared because of Love.
   All shines from Love.
   All pulses from Love.
   All flows from Love.
No, once again all is Love!

    Fakhruddin Araqi. Translated by Jonathan Star.

On Christianity

He who is thus a spiritual lover knows well what that voice means which says: "You, Lord God, are my whole love and desire. You are all mine, and I all Yours. Dissolve my heart into Your love so that I may know how sweet it is to serve You and how joyful it is to praise You, and to be as though I were all melded into Your love.... I shall sing to you the song of Love … and my soul will never be weary in praising You with the joyful songs of unconditional love."

    Saint Thomas á Kempis

Let nothing disturb thee,
Nothing affright thee;
All things are passing;
God never changeth;
Patient endurance
Attaineth to all things;
Who God possesseth
In nothing is wanting;
Alone God sufficeth.

> *Saint Teresa of Avila.*
> *Translated by Henry Wadsworth Longfellow.*

These lines were written on a bookmark
found in her breviary.

Praise the Lord: Psalm 150

Praise the Lord!
Praise God in his sanctuary;
Praise him in the firmament of his power
Praise him for his mighty acts;
Praise him according to his greatness!
Praise him with the sound of the trumpet;
Praise him with the psaltery and harp.
Praise him with the timbrel and dance;
Praise him with stringed instruments and pipes;
Praise him upon the crashing cymbals.
Let everything that has breath praise the Lord!
    Hallelujah!

Call to Worship

Let us sing a new song to the Lord,
The Lord of our lives and of all creation,
The Lord in whose image we have been created.
Let us sing of repentance and return to truth reality.
Let us sing to educate the consciousness of Oneness
    to all people.
Let us sing to kindle hope and joy in humanity.
Let us sing to move the nations to positive, open interaction.
Let us sing to celebrate the Spirit of the Lord,
Working deep in the heart of our time.
Let us sing of pure divine love and precious humility
Of the souls whose sincere desire is to realize its oneness
    with God.

Rebekah Dunlap

The Heaven of Ancient Egypt

I have heard those songs which are inscribed in the ancient sepulchres and what they tell in praise of life on earth and belittling the region of the dead. Yet wherefore do they this in regard to the land of Eternity, the just and the fair, where fear is not? Wrangling is its abhorrence, nor does any there gird himself against his fellow. That land, free of enemies!—all our kinsmen from the earliest days of time rest within it. The children of millions of millions come thither, everyone. For none may tarry in the land of Egypt; none there is that passeth not thither. The span of our earthly deeds is as a dream; but fair is the welcome that awaits him who has reached the hills of the West.

Neferhotep

Book of Ecclesiasticus

He was as the morning star in the midst of a cloud, and as the moon at the full: As the sun shining upon the temple of the most High, and as the rainbow giving light in the bright clouds: And as the flower of roses in the spring of the year, as lilies by the rivers of water, and as the branches of the frankincense tree in the time of summer: As fire and incense in the censer, and as a vessel of beaten gold set with all manner of precious stones: And as a fair olive tree budding forth fruit, and as a cypress tree which groweth up to the clouds. When he put on the robe of honour, and was clothed with the perfection of glory, when he went up to the holy altar, he made the garment of holiness honourable.

Loving Your Neighbor

Love is like light. In fact, light is one of its manifestations. Scientists have discovered that light is complete in and of itself. It is not something existing in something else. It is not dependent on anything else. It doesn't draw its nature from anything else. It is light, and it shines because it is light. It acts out of its own nature and is not concerned because it shines on a very dark night or in a dark room.

Jesus used the sun to illustrate the nature of love. He said it shines on the just and on the unjust and pointed out that the rain falls on the deserving and on the undeserving alike. A delightful story is told about how the sun and the lesser ones in the heavens got together to discuss the darkness on earth.

Several had gone down and reported tremendous darkness in many areas. The sun said, "I will go down to the earth and see for myself," and then returned to report to the others that it had not been able to find a single dark spot on the earth. The sun shines because it is the sun, and love loves because it is love. So, too, it is with the one who is learning to be true to his real self. He loves because he is love. He lives because he is life. He shines because he is light, and he laughs because he is joy. He acts not in conformity or rebellion, but because he is true to himself— a creature of love, life, light, and laughter. He is a Spiritual Independent, neither deflated nor inflated by the opinions, actions, or postures of others, real or imaginary. He is learning to be true to the integrity, or nature, of his own inner being.

J. Sig Paulson

Pray remember what I have recommended to you, which is, to think often on God, by day, by night, in your business, and even in your diversions. He is always near you and with you; leave Him not alone. You would think it rude to leave a friend alone who came to visit you: why then must God be neglected? Do not then forget Him, but think on Him often, adore Him continually, live and die with Him; this is the glorious employment of a Christian; in a word, this is our profession; if we do not know it we must learn it. I will endeavour to help you with my prayers.

Brother Lawrence

How Would It Be?

How would it be
if just for today
we thought less about contests and rivalries,
profits and politics,
winners and sinners,
and more about helping and giving,
mending and blending,
reaching out
and pitching in?
How would it be?

Anonymous

What Are You Doing?

Today, this moment, right now is the most important time you have. Tomorrow is for the one who would not now do what can be done. Tomorrow is for the one who is without interest. Where there is interest, there is activity and transformation. How beautifully Paul said this when he declared, "Be not conformed to this world but be transformed by the renewal of your mind, that you may prove what is the will of God, what is good and acceptable and perfect" (Rom. 12:2).

Will you accept the challenge and the change—and transform yourself?

The earnest person is one who is completely dedicated to the task at hand. There is simplicity in what we seek to do when we dedicate ourself to the doing. At this moment accept only what uplifts, but don't reject what you do not understand. In a definite change of attitude, embrace all things that are part of you. Then release—release all and everything.

Become still and know. Know that order, *divine order*, is the higher Self expressing through an expanded conscious awareness of you, your world, and your part in it. Make no intense effort to determine the "how" or "why." Accept. Relax. Release. In this moment there can be an enlightenment of you as an individual, and all else and all others may emerge in the light of a new and brighter dawn.

Spiritual development is not the result of a desperate effort to be good: rather, it is an inward realization of right thinking, feeling, and action that can transmute the whole nature into the likeness and reality of Truth. There can be no transformation in body or affairs until there is transformation within our mind. Expansion of consciousness and greater expression of all that is good can result from quiet, contemplative moments of meditation and devoted prayer.

Rebecca Clark

Blessings at Year End

I remember with gratitude the fruits of the labors of others, which I have shared as part of the normal experience of daily living.

I remember the beautiful things that I have seen, heard, and felt—some, as a result of definite seeking on my part, and many that came unheralded into my path, warming my heart and rejoicing my spirit.

I remember the moments of distress that proved to be groundless and those that taught me profoundly about the evilness of evil and the goodness of good.

I remember the new people I have met, from whom I have caught glimpses of the meaning of my own life and the true character of human dignity.

I remember the dreams that haunted me during the year, keeping me ever mindful of goals and hopes which I did not realize but from which I drew inspiration to sustain my life and keep steady my purpose.

I remember the awareness of the spirit of God that sought me out in my aloneness and gave to me a sense of assurance that undercut my despair and confirmed my life with new courage and abiding hope.

Howard Thurman

Reading List

Baha'i Prayers. Wilmette, Ill.: Baha'i Publishing Trust, 1991.

Buell, Lawrence, ed. *Henry Wadsworth Longfellow: Selected Poems.* New York: Penguin Books, 1988.

Church, F. Forrester, and Terrence J. Mulry, eds. *The Macmillan Book of Earliest Christian Hymns.* New York: Macmillan, 1988.

Clark, Rebecca. *Breakthrough.* Unity Village, Mo.: Unity Books, 1977.

———. *The Rainbow Connection.* Unity Village, Mo.: Unity Books, 1983.

Cole, W. Owen, and V. P. (Hemant) Kanitkar. *Hinduism.* Lincolnwood, Ill.: NTC Publishing Group, 1995.

The Complete Poems of Carl Sandburg. Introduction by Archibald MacLeish. New York: Harcourt Brace Jovanovich, 1969.

Complete Poems of Robert Frost. New York: Holt, Rinehart and Winston, 1949.

Craughwell, Thomas J., ed. *Every Eye Beholds You.* New York: Quality Paperback Book Club, 1998.

Dunn, Philip, comp. *Prayer: Language of the Soul.* New York: Dell, 1997.

The Essential Rumi. Trans. Coleman Barks with John Moyne, A. J. Arberry, and Reynold Nicholson. New York: HarperCollins, 1995.

Feldman, Christina, and Jack Kornfield, eds. *Stories of the Spirit: Stories of the Heart.* New York: HarperCollins, 1991.

Ford-Grabowsky, Mary. *Sacred Poems and Prayers of Love.* New York: Doubleday, 1998.

Fox, Emmet. *Alter Your Life.* New York: Harper and Row, 1931.

———. *Make Your Life Worthwhile*. New York: Harper and Row, 1942.

Freeman, James Dillet. *What God Is Like*. Unity Village, Mo.: Unity Books, 1973.

Gaer, Joseph, ed. *What the Great Religions Believe*. New York: Dodd, Mead, 1963.

Gesner, George, ed. *Anthology of American Poetry*. New York: Avenel Books, 1983.

Goudge, Elizabeth. *A Book of Comfort*. New York: Coward-McCann, 1964.

Gribetz, Jessica, ed. *Wise Words*. New York: William Morrow, 1997.

Krishnamurti, J. *Think on These Things*. Edited by D. Rajagopal. New York: Harper and Row, 1964.

Mbiti, John S. *The Prayers of the African Religion*. Maryknoll, N.Y.: Orbis Books, 1975.

Mennonite Church Hymnal. Scottsdale, Pa.: Mennonite Publishing House, 1927.

Mennonite Hymnal. Scottsdale, Pa.: Herald Press, 1969.

Mitchell, Stephen, ed. *The Enlightened Heart: An Anthology of Sacred Poetry*. New York: Harper and Row, 1989.

———. *The Enlightened Mind*. New York: HarperCollins, 1991.

Moore, Gerald, and Ulli Beier, eds. *Modern African Poetry*. New York: Penguin, 1984.

Muktananda. *Play of Consciousness*. Oakland, Calif.: SYDA Foundation, 1978.

New Light in the Dawn. Unity Village, Mo.: Unity Books, 1990.

Novak, Philip, ed. *The World's Wisdom: Sacred Texts of the World's Religions*. New York: HarperCollins, 1994.

Paulson, J. Sig. *How to Love Your Neighbor*. New York: Doubleday, 1974.

Peale, Norman Vincent. *A Treasury of Joy and Enthusiasm*. Old Tappan, N.J.: Fleming H. Revell, 1981.

Rinpoche, Sogyal. *Glimpse After Glimpse*. New York: HarperCollins, 1995.

————. *The Tibetan Book of Living and Dying*. New York: Harper-Collins, 1993.

Ryan, M. J., ed. *A Grateful Heart*. Berkeley, Calif.: Conari Press, 1994.

Seaburg, Carl, ed. *Great Occasions*. Boston: Beacon Press, 1968.

A Shaker Hymnal. New York: Overlook Press, 1996.

Singing the Living Tradition. Boston: Beacon Press, 1992.

Strong, Mary. *Letters of the Scattered Brotherhood*. New York: Harper and Row, 1948.

Teilhard de Chardin, Pierre. *The Future of Man*. New York: Harper and Row, 1964.

Templeton, John Marks. *The Humble Approach*. Philadelphia, Pa.: Templeton Foundation Press, 1981, 1995.

————. *Worldwide Laws of Life*. Philadelphia, Pa.: Templeton Foundation Press, 1998.

————, ed. *Riches for the Mind and Spirit*. New York: HarperCollins, 1990.

Templeton, John Marks, and Robert L. Herrmann. *Is God the Only Reality?* New York: Continuum, 1994.

Trine, Ralph Waldo. *In Tune with the Infinite*. Indianapolis: Bobbs-Merrill, 1908.

Truth the Poet Sings. Unity Village, Mo.: Unity Books, 1984.

Wilber, Ken. *Grace and Grit*. Boston: Shambhala, 1991.

Williams, Oscar, and Edwin Honig, eds. *Major American Poets*. New York: Penguin, 1962.

Williams, Paul. *Das Energi*. Encinitas, Calif.: Entwhistle Books, 1973.

Wings of Song Hymnal. Unity Village, Mo.: Unity Books, 1984.

Wonderful You. Unity Village, Mo.: Unity Books, 1976.

Author Index

Faber, Frederick W. (1814–63; Evangelical clergyman and author), 90
Fillmore, Lowell (b. 1882), 184
Fillmore, Myrtle (1845–1931), 137
Fox, Emmet, 209, 228
Francis of Assisi, Saint (1182–1226; founder of Franciscan order),
    17–18, 224
Freeman, James Dillet, 135, 141, 147–48, 153
Frost, Robert (1874–1963; U.S. poet), 16, 156–58

Gandhi, Mohandas Karamchand (Mahatma, 1869–1948;
    Indian spiritual and political leader), 165
Gannett, William Channing (1840–1923), 99
Ghose, Aurobindo (1872–1950; Indian metaphysician), 30
Gibran, Kahlil (1883–1931; Syrian/Lebanese writer), 29, 154
Giovanni, Fra (c. 1433–1515), 230
Gordon, A. D. (1856–1922), 244
Gregory Nazianzus, Saint (329–89; Church father), 221
Gregory the Great (c. 540–604), 63
Guest, Edgar A. (1881–1959; English/U.S. poet), 146

Hatton, John (1710–93), 74
Herbert, George (1593–1633; English priest and poet), 123
Hildegard of Bingen (1098–1179; German abbess and visionary), 165
Hille, Waldemar (1908–), 84
Hintze, Jacob, 104
Hirshfield, Jane, 178
Holmes, John (1904–62), 102
Holmes, Oliver Wendell (1809–94; U.S. writer and physician), 127
Hull, Eleanor H. (1860–1935), 73
Hyde, William DeWitt (1858–1917), 80

Ibn 'Arabi (1165–1240; Sufi mystic), 40
Ide, Beth (1921–), 80
Iqbal, Sir Mohammed (1877–1938; Islamic poet and philosopher),
    204
Ireland, John (1879–1962; English composer and pianist), 78
Isa Upanishad, 220

Muhammad (570–632; prophet of Islam), 21, 250
Muir, Edwin (1887–1959), 251
Muktananda, Swami Paramahamsa (1908–), 243–44

Neferhotep, 258

Oliver, William E., 84

Paulson, J. Sig, 260
Pierpoint, Folliott Sanford (1835–1917), 61
Prichard, Rowland H. (1811–87), 60

Quimada, Bishop Toribio, 76–77

Ramakrishna (1836–86; Hindu mystic), 215
Rilke, Rainer Maria (1875–1926; German lyric poet), 150
Rinpoche, Sogyal, 206, 227, 250
Roberts, John, 103
Ross, Robert A. M. (1955–), 62, 70–71, 76–77, 97, 105
Rowan, William P. (1951–), 100–101
Rumi, Jalal al-Din (1207–73; Persian poet), 32, 235–36, 238, 239
Russell, Janna, 133
Rutledge, Horace, 160

Sa'ib of Tabriz (c. 1601–77; Persian poet), 37
Sadat, Anwar (1918–81; Egyptian military and political leader), 250
Sandburg, Carl (1878–1967; U.S. poet), 155
Santayana, George (1863–1952; Spanish philosopher), 159
Saxe, John Godfrey (1816–87; U.S. attorney and writer), 128, 174–75
Schopenhauer, Arthur, 220
Sibelius, Jean (1865–1957; Finnish composer), 82–83
Singh, Sadhu Sundar (1889–c. 1929), 170
Smart, Henry, 99
Smit, Leo (1921– ; U.S. composer and pianist), 113
Smith, Walter Chalmers (1824–1908), 103
Stanford, Charles V. (1852–1924), 119
Star, Jonathan, 254

Wordsworth, William (1770–1850; English poet), 138–39
Wren, Brian (1936–), 100–101, 105
Wright, Samuel Anthony (1919–), 82–83
Wyeth, John, 98

Yogananda, Paramahansa, 13, 44
Young, Carlton R. (1926–), 73

Zundel, John (1815–82), 86–87

First Line, or Title, Index

ACKNOWLEDGMENTS

PAGE

8   "In the Beginning Was God," from John S. Mbiti, *The Prayers of the African Religion* (Maryknoll, N.Y.: Orbis Books, 1975). Used by permission of the author.

9   "Prayer for Mankind," from *Bahá'i Prayers* 1954 © 1996 by the National Spiritual Assembly of the Bahá'is of the United States. Reprinted with permission of the publisher, the Bahá'i Publishing Trust, Wilmette, IL.

10 "i thank You God for most this amazing." Copyright 1950, © 1978, 1991 by the Trustees for the E. E. Cummings Trust. Copyright © 1979 by George James Firmage, from *Complete Poems: 1904-1962* by E. E. Cummings, edited by George J. Firmage. Used by permission of Liveright Publishing Corporation.

20 "A Prayer," from *Francis and Clare: The Complete Works* (Mahwah, N.J.: Paulist Press, 1982). Used by permission of the publisher.

22 "Let me not pray, . . ." Reprinted with the permission of Scribner, a Division of Simon & Schuster from *The Collected Poems and Plays of Rabindranath Tagore* (New York: Macmillan, 1937).

24 "Prayer for Assistance," from *Bahá'i Prayers* 1954 © 1996 by the National Spiritual Assembly of the Bahá'is of the United States. Reprinted with permission of the publisher, the Bahá'i Publishing Trust, Wilmette, IL.

28 "For a Day Full of Blessings," from John S. Mbiti, *The Prayers of the African Religion* (Maryknoll, N.Y.: Orbis Books, 1975). Used by permission of the author.

31 "Prayer for Detachment," from *Bahá'i Prayers* 1954 © 1996 by the National Spiritual Assembly of the Bahá'is of the United States. Reprinted with permission of the publisher, the Bahá'i Publishing Trust, Wilmette, IL.

32 "Prayer for Forgiveness," from *Bahá'i Prayers* 1954 © 1996 by the National Spiritual Assembly of the Bahá'is of the United States. Reprinted with permission of the publisher, the Bahá'i Publishing Trust, Wilmette, IL.

38 "Prayer for Spiritual Qualities," from *Bahá'i Prayers* 1954, © 1996 by the National Spiritual Assembly of the Bahá'is of the United States. Reprinted with permission of the publisher, the Bahá'i Publishing Trust, Wilmette, IL.

40 "Universal Tolerance," from *Mystical Dimensions of Islam* by Annemarie Schimmel. Copyright © 1975 by the University of North Carolina Press. Used by permission of the publisher.

45 "A Prayer of White Eagle," reprinted with permission of White Eagle Publishing, Hants, England.

86 "Love Divine." Copied from *Mennonite Hymnal,* © 1969 by Herald Press, Scottdale, PA 15683. Used by permission.

88 "Sweet Hour of Prayer." Copied from *Mennonite Hymnal,* © 1969 by Herald Press, Scottdale, PA 15683. Used by permission.

90 "O God, Thy Power Is Wonderful." Copied from *Mennonite Hymnal,* © 1927, renewed 1955 by Mennonite Press, Scottdale, PA 15683. Used by permission.

113 Emily Dickinson, "If I Can Stop One Heart from Breaking," reprinted by permission of the publishers and the Trustees of Amherst College from *The Poems of Emily Dickinson,* Thomas H. Johnson, ed., Cambridge, Mass.: The Belknap Press of Harvard University Press, Copyright © 1951, 1955, 1979, 1983 by the President and Fellows of Harvard College.

124 "Every being in the universe," from *Tao Te Ching by Lao Tzu: A New English Version, with Foreword and Notes by Stephen Mitchell.* Translation copyright © 1988 by Stephen Mitchell. Reprinted with permission of HarperCollins Publishers, Inc.

133 "Eternal Love," from *Truth the Poet Sings.* Used with permission of Unity School of Christianity, 1901 NW Blue Parkway, Unity Village, MO 64065.

134   "What Is Love," from *Truth the Poet Sings*. Used with permission of Unity School of Christianity, 1901 NW Blue Parkway, Unity Village, MO 64065.

135   "What God Is Like," from *What God Is Like*. Used with permission of Unity School of Christianity, 1901 NW Blue Parkway, Unity Village, MO 64065.

136   "God Spoke to Me," from *Truth the Poet Sings*. Used with permission of Unity School of Christianity, 1901 NW Blue Parkway, Unity Village, MO 64065.

137   "My Love to Thee," from *Truth the Poet Sings*. Used with permission of Unity School of Christianity, 1901 NW Blue Parkway, Unity Village, MO 64065.

141   "God Is in the Midst of Me," from *What God Is Like*. Used with permission of Unity School of Christianity, 1901 NW Blue Parkway, Unity Village, MO 64065.

145   "The Vision," from *The Rainbow Connection*. Used with permission of Unity School of Christianity, 1901 NW Blue Parkway, Unity Village, MO 64065.

147   "I Am There," from *What God Is Like*. Used with permission of Unity School of Christianity, 1901 NW Blue Parkway, Unity Village, MO 64065.

150   "As once the wingèd energy of delight . . ." From *The Selected Poetry of Rainer Maria Rilke*. Edited and translated by Stephen Mitchell. Copyright © 1982 by Stephen Mitchell. Reprinted by permission of Random House, Inc.

153   James Dillet Freeman, "What Lies Beyond," from *What God Is Like*. Used with permission of Unity School of Christianity, 1901 NW Blue Parkway, Unity Village, MO 64065.

155   Carl Sandburg, "Glass House Canticle," from *The Complete Poems of Carl Sandburg*, copyright © 1970, 1969 by Lilian Steichen Sandburg, Trustee, reprinted by permission of Harcourt, Inc.

161   "Precious Seed," from *Wonderful You*. Used with permission of Unity School of Christianity, 1901 NW Blue Parkway, Unity Village, MO 64065.

right © 1988 by Stephen Mitchell. Reprinted with permission of HarperCollins Publishers, Inc.

181 "Affirmation of a Seeking Heart," from *The Rainbow Connection*. Used with permission of Unity School of Christianity, 1901 NW Blue Parkway, Unity Village, MO 64065.

182 "Within the Depths of Me," from *New Light in the Dawn*. Used with permission of Unity School of Christianity, 1901 NW Blue Parkway, Unity Village, MO 64065.

183 "Birth—Awareness," from *Truth the Poet Sings*. Used with permission of Unity School of Christianity, 1901 NW Blue Parkway, Unity Village, MO 64065.

184 "The Answer," from *Truth the Poet Sings*. Used with permission of Unity School of Christianity, 1901 NW Blue Parkway, Unity Village, MO 64065.

189 "Listen!" from *The Circle of God's Love*. Used with permission of Unity School of Christianity, 1901 NW Blue Parkway, Unity Village, MO 64065.

205 Excerpt from *Think on These Things* by J. Krishnamurti. Copyright © 1964 by the Krishnamurti Foundation of America. Copyright renewed. Reprinted by permission of HarperCollins Publishers, Inc.

206 No. 3/1 from *Glimpse after Glimpse* by Sogyal Rinpoche. Copyright © 1995 by Sogyal Rinpoche. Reprinted by permission of HarperCollins Publishers, Inc.

208 Excerpt from *Think on These Things* by J. Krishnamurti. Copyright © 1964 by the Krishnamurti Foundation of America. Copyright renewed. Reprinted by permission of HarperCollins Publishers, Inc.

209 "A Smile Is an Investment," from *Make Your Life Worthwhile* by Emmet Fox. Copyright 1942, 1943, 1944, 1945, 1946 by Emmet Fox. Copyright renewed © 1974 by Kathleen Whelan. Reprinted by permission of HarperCollins Publishers, Inc.

214 "Be Like a Child," from *Letters of the Scattered Brotherhood* by Mary Strong. Copyright 1948 by Harper & Brothers, renewed © 1975 by George W. Penny Jr. Reprinted by permission of HarperCollins Publishers, Inc.

227 "How to Awaken Love and Compassion," from *The Tibetan Book of Living and Dying* by Sogyal Rinpoche. Copyright © 1993 by Rigpa Fellowship. Reprinted by permission of HarperCollins Publishers, Inc.

228 "Keep on the Beam," from *Alter Your Life* by Emmet Fox. Copyright 1950 by Emmet Fox; renewed © 1978 by Kathleen Whelan. Reprinted by permission of HarperCollins Publishers, Inc.

234 Gerald Jampolsky, "My whole being pulsates . . .," excerpted from *A Grateful Heart* by M. J. Ryan, copyright © 1994 by M. J. Ryan, by permission of Conari Press.

235 Rumi, "Father Reason," from *The Essential Rumi,* trans. Coleman Barks with John Moyne, A. J. Arberry, and Reynold Nicholson (San Francisco: HarperSanFrancisco, 1995). Reprinted by permission of Threshold Books.

237 Excerpts from *Think on These Things* by J. Krishnamurti. Copyright © 1964 by the Krishnamurti Foundation of America. Copyright renewed. Reprinted by permission of HarperCollins Publishers, Inc.

238 Rumi, "Only Breath," from *The Essential Rumi,* trans. Coleman Barks with John Moyne, A. J. Arberry, and Reynold Nicholson (San Francisco: HarperSanFrancisco, 1995). Reprinted by permission of Threshold Books.

239 Rumi, "In your light, . . ." from *The Essential Rumi,* trans. Coleman Barks with John Moyne, A. J. Arberry, and Reynold Nicholson (San Francisco: HarperSanFrancisco, 1995). Reprinted by permission of Threshold Books.

243 "The Path of Love," excerpt from Chapter 39 of the third edition of Swami Muktananda's *Play of Consciousness,* pp. 265-66. Copyright © 2000 SYDA Foundation. All rights reserved. Reprinted by permission.

260 From *How to Love Your Neighbor* by J. Sig Paulson. Copyright © 1974 by J. Sig Paulson. Used by permission of Doubleday, a division of Random House, Inc.